Beginning Drama 11–14

SECOND EDITION

Related titles

Speaking, Listening and Drama, Andy Kempe and Jan Holroyd

Starting Drama Teaching, Mike Fleming

The Art of Drama Teaching, Mike Fleming

Beginning Drama 11–14

SECOND EDITION

Jonothan Neelands

 David Fulton Publishers

This edition reprinted 2008 by Routledge
2 Park Square, Milton Park, Abingdon, Oxon OX14 4RN
Simultaneously published in the USA and Canada
By Routledge
270 Madison Avenue, New York, NY 10016

First published in Great Britain in 1998 by David Fulton Publishers

British Library Cataloguing in Publication Data
A catalogue record for this book is available from the British Library.

ISBN 1 84312 086 0

Typeset by FiSH Books, London

Contents

Acknowledgements

This book is dedicated to *the usual suspects* – you know who you are and will recognise your influence throughout these pages. A special thanks to Gavin Bolton, David Booth, Warwick Dobson and Fred Inglis for their acts of solidarity during the thesis writing. Thanks to David Booth and Mike Fleming for suggesting this book. Thanks also to Judith Ackroyd and Jo Trowsdale for their critical reading of early drafts.

I hope that those friends, teachers and PGCE pupils who remain unnamed will realise how much I have needed their time and support in this as in every project.

Introduction to the Second Edition

The first edition of *Beginning Drama 11–14* was a response to the growth of drama as a subject in its own right in Key Stage 3. At that time there was very little guidance for new and experienced specialist teachers of drama. In particular, the first edition drew attention to the problems of assessment and planning for progression in a drama curriculum.

In the last few years there have been a number of new publications for drama teachers that have further informed approaches and practice in the areas of assessment and progression. Andy Kempe's and Marigold Ashwell's *Progression in Secondary Drama*[1], for instance, has provided us with a detailed map of progression, and clear suggestions for assessing pupils based on levels of achievement.

Recently there have been a number of new guidance documents for drama at KS3 published by various government departments and agencies. These documents also reflect the continuing growth of drama in secondary schools in England, and the important connections between drama and other key government initiatives such as the National Literacy Strategy, the KS3 Strategy and the Citizenship Curriculum.

This new, second edition of *Beginning Drama 11–14* has been written in response to the new guidance documents and publications, such as *Progression in Secondary Drama*. In particular, it is designed to complement *The Drama Objectives Bank*,[2] published by the KS3 National Strategy. In the absence of statutory orders for drama, this document will play a key role in guiding specialist teachers of drama to design, teach and assess a KS3 drama curriculum.

Section One: The Drama Curriculum has been rewritten to offer a new and detailed curriculum model based on *The Drama Objectives Bank* and other new guidance documents, and updated to include new understandings about progression and assessment in drama. Section Three: Resources has three new sequences of lessons for KS3, and updated bibliographies.

This edition also seeks to re-emphasise the importance of linking and valuing the social and aesthetic dimensions of teaching and learning in drama. Drama teachers, rightly, want to see drama established as an arts subject in its own right in the curriculum, rather than as an adjunct of English. But it is important also that drama teachers do not separate and distance themselves from the vital cultural and social agendas which are shared with English and the

---

[1] Kempe, A. & Ashwell, M. (2000) *Progression in Secondary Drama*, Heinemann.
[2] www.standards.dfes.gov.uk/keystages

Humanities in general. Drama is, in my view, a subject without walls. It can make a rich contribution to other subjects, be enriched by including pedagogic practices and ideas developed in other subject areas, and lead the new cross-curricular emphasis on developing high-quality teaching and learning approaches which underpin all good practice, irrespective of subject boundaries.

Preface

Welcome to drama!

This is the second book in a series which is designed for pupil-teachers, non-specialist teachers who have an interest in knowing more and specialist teachers of drama who might need refreshing! In *Beginning Drama: 4–11* Joe Winston and Miles Tandy considered the role of drama in the primary phases of education. They described the role of drama as a medium for learning in many subjects of the primary school curriculum and laid out the beginnings of a course of study of drama as a subject. In that first book, the audience is assumed to be classroom teachers with a general responsibility for the whole curriculum including drama. Now, in this second book, we build on the advice and model of drama offered in the first book and move forward to the first years of secondary schooling. The key difference is that now we are considering drama as a specialist subject in the school curriculum, taught by a specialist teacher.

Some readers may be surprised by the scope, detail and complexity of some sections in this book. It is, after all, a beginners' guide. In our view it is important to begin with the idea that drama is a specialist subject that has its own curriculum framework, skills, concepts and knowledge. That is what this book tries to do – to introduce you to the foundations of knowledge, skills and experiences which together constitute the specialist study and practice of drama. It is quite possible to teach drama in the middle years without some of the specialisms described in this book, but we assume that you want to do more than follow other people's recipes without knowing, for yourself, how drama works.

The emphasis on drama as a subject in this book means that it has tried to cover, and integrate where possible, all that a specialist teacher might be asked to know and do. It assumes for instance, that a specialist will provide three dimensions of drama in the school: as curriculum subject; as extra-curricular activity; and as community performance. There is also an emphasis on the long-term planning of curriculum objectives, progression and continuity, and assessment across the middle years and in preparation for the advanced study of drama in later years.

The book is written as a practical guide, or subject handbook; there are no references or quotations from other sources or to the extensive body of research that contributes to the ideas expressed. It is written as a synthesis of the drama education theories and practices that have been developed over the last two decades or more. I have tried to represent the richness of a community of teachers, researchers and theorists working in many different countries and contexts. Many of these people are represented in the bibliographies in the *Resources* section which also contains annotated guides to specialist drama education texts and resources. The bibliography is intended to guide you once you have completed this book.

Can this be drama?

For those of you who are new to teaching, your first experiences of drama in schools may offer a few surprises. The forms of drama to be found in schools often look and feel very different from the theatre experiences we have out of school. (You might want to look through some of the lesson structures contained in the *Resources* section before reading on if you are unfamiliar with school drama.) Why should this be?

In the popular imagination theatre is often thought of as the performance of plays by professional or amateur actors to a paying audience. It is a picture of theatre that is based on an economic agreement between the producers and the audience. The producers rehearse and develop a theatre product to the best of their abilities and, when the time comes, they perform their work in exchange for the price of a ticket.

More often than not the product that is exchanged is based on the work of a playwright. There is an assumption in this model of theatre that the majority of us will see, rather than be in, such plays. Acting, producing theatre, is seen as something only a few can achieve. There is also the assumption that the audience in this literary theatre will be silent and attentive to the work of the actors – audience responses are private rather than publicly shared as they might be in more popular forms of entertainment. I refer to theatre that corresponds to this image as belonging to the **literary and private aesthetic tradition**. If this popular image of theatre is the dominant one in most Western societies, it should be remembered that there are alternative models of community theatre and performance which may bring us closer to recognising drama-making in schools as theatre.

In local communities in our society and in many traditional societies, the arts still serve the important civic and community functions that ritual and art-making once provided for us all. In the golden ages of Athenian and Elizabethan drama, for instance, going to the theatre was an important and integral part of the public life of the citizen. The theatre still offers communities a public forum for debating, affirming and challenging culture and community ties. In this community model, the arts are seen as important means of representing and commenting on the cultural life and beliefs of the community; in turn, the communal participation of the whole community in art-making strengthens their cultural bonds. Every member of the group is seen as a potential producer – a potential artist. In this model, theatre is produced on the basis of a social agreement between members of a group who come together to make something that will be of importance to them: something that will signify their lives.

Drama that is produced on the basis of a social contract is likely to be local in its effect – its 'meanings' belong to the group who produces them and are addressed to the group as a whole. Because the live experience of communal performance is most important, such performances tend not to be recorded as play scripts – they are orally created and remembered. For this reason, communal drama belongs to what I will call the **oral and communal aesthetic tradition** which stresses the processes of production and the quality for participants of the immediate shared experience. The oral and communal tradition of non-literary and participatory entertainment is familiar to pupils from their experience of popular sports and entertainments and from their own community experiences of communal dancing, singing, storytelling and rituals.

This alternative social and community model of theatre shares some of the characteristics of drama in schools. A school is a community and drama is a living practice within it. The drama that young people make is often based on the concerns, needs and aspirations shared within the school community, or the community of a particular teaching group. It is often based on a social agreement that all who are present are potential producers – everyone can have a go at being actors and/or audience as the drama progresses. The coming together to make drama is also often seen as an important means of making the teaching group more conscious of themselves as a living community.

The forms that drama takes in school may also appear strangely different. There may be bewildering references to *tableau, hot-seating, thought-tracking*. This difference is partly due to the emphasis on joining in and making drama, so that many of these terms refer to ways in which drama can be made rather than watched. It is also due to a more pragmatic cause. Drama is taught in short periods of time, awkward spaces, to large numbers of pupils who are not all committed to doing it! These are not the conditions in which professional theatre is made. Drama teachers have developed ways of working and conventions that provide pupils with theatre experiences within these constraints. This book hopes to establish the theatrical foundations of this school-based version of drama and to show how it can lead to the study of theatre in other forms and contexts. This is the wonder of theatre, that a rich and multi-faceted variety of forms, conventions, genres and traditions have been spawned in response to the different needs and cultures of the contexts where it is produced.

ENJOY!

Ages and stages

This book covers the drama curriculum for pupils aged between 11 and 14. The references to Key Stages (KS) and Years reflect the English education system. The following guide is for readers who may be unfamiliar with this system.

Key Stage	Year	Age
KS1	1	5–6
	2	6–7
	3	7–8
KS2	4	8–9
	5	9–10
	6	10–11
KS3	7	11–12
	8	12–13
	9	13–14
KS4 (GCSE)	10	14–15
	11	15–16
POST-16	12	16–17
	13	17–18

1

The drama curriculum

How do we begin to plan a drama curriculum for the middle years? In this chapter we will consider the issues and elements of such a curriculum. This will include some discussion about what should be included and excluded, leading to a definition of theatre and the framing of aims and objectives. Further sections give advice on the principles of progression and continuity which might underpin the drama curriculum and suggest a framework for assessing pupils' achievements in drama.

The chapter closes with notes on the important relationship between drama and language development and a reminder of the vital role that drama can play in young people's lives and in the life of the school.

The field of drama

What should a drama curriculum cover? What are its priorities in the middle years of schooling? What will pupils be expected to know, understand and be able to do?

In our world, the term 'drama' is used to refer to a diverse range of cultural practices which range from dramatic literature through to dramatic events in the news. In between we find the drama of TV and film, live theatre and the lived dramas of our personal and social lives. In our 'dramatised society' what is to be selected from the field of drama for inclusion and exclusion in a curriculum for drama?

The problem of making a selection from all the possibles in the contemporary field of drama is compounded by the problem of making a selection from the past. Whose histories and traditions do we include? There are obvious problems, in our pluralist and multicultural classrooms, in limiting the history of drama to those writers and practitioners who have contributed to the development of the modern Western theatre. The Western conventional theatre of the last hundred years or so has developed as a literary art, increasingly restricted to particular social groups and increasingly differentiated from other genres of popular drama and entertainment. Its selective tradition is often told in a form that suggests that the conventional theatre of our time is the natural evolution from earlier and inferior sources, particularly from the oral and communal traditions of performance. What messages does this send to pupils from cultures that have living performance traditions that are different? What does it tell pupils whose social and cultural history is different from that of the middle-class theatre audience?

What it is that we are preparing pupils to do in drama? In English, pupils become literate and effective speakers, listeners, readers and writers. In music and dance we prepare them to be players, dancers and critical audiences, but in drama there is an even wider range of roles that we might prepare them for: playwrights, dramaturges, actors, designers, technicians, directors, stage managers. Drama is the most social of all art forms; it uses a range of diverse skills and roles in its production. The range of roles is further extended when film and TV production are included in the drama curriculum.

Beyond these roles, there are also the roles and skills associated with the pupils' own use of drama, both in the classroom and in school performances and extra-curricular drama clubs. The participatory and cooperative forms of theatre that have become associated with the practice of drama in schools require pupils to be effective negotiators, group members, researchers and devisers in addition to the conventional roles described above.

How can a drama curriculum cover so much?

Traditionally, approaches to curriculum planning in drama have tended to distinguish between 'theatre' and 'drama' In this distinction, 'theatre' is often taken to mean the study of the literature and practices of those conventional forms of professional and amateur theatre which have become associated with middle-class Western audiences (the literary and private aesthetic tradition). When this conception of 'theatre' operates, the emphasis is often on the formal study of the achievements of playwrights and on the skills needed to understand and appreciate their work in performance.

'Drama' on the other hand is taken to mean the practice of improvised and participatory forms of drama, which often derive their essentially oral and communal aesthetic from popular forms of entertainment. The practice of 'drama' is often seen as serving important and immediate personal and social purposes in young people's lives.

The problem with this historical distinction in drama education is that it drives an unnecessary wedge between two living traditions, or genres, of performance which ought to be studied and practised in harmony. Theatre can be both the literary professional theatre and the popular oral and communal theatre. It is part of the wonder of the art that it has developed so many different forms in response to the living contexts in which it is made and responded to. Theatre is one aspect of the cultural field of drama, but theatre is also a field in which there are many different positions, traditions, genres and histories.

There will always be problems with a drama curriculum that creates an imbalance between these exclusive concepts of 'theatre' and 'drama' and the aesthetic traditions that they represent. An emphasis on a socially restricted concept of 'theatre' may ignore many pupils' own experiences and everyday knowledge of drama and other forms of popular entertainment and may ignore the important contribution that drama education can make to their own living experiences of the worlds in which they live.

To ignore the literary theatre tradition also results in exclusion. Knowledge and understanding of how such theatre is produced and how it is understood and fully appreciated is not generally available to all social and cultural groups. It has been historically restricted to those of a certain education and upbringing. For many pupils, school is the place where they too can be introduced to and enjoy the pleasures of the literary theatre while becoming conscious of its particular social history.

We need the kind of balance that many English teachers struggle for between reading and appreciating novels and the literary heritage, for instance, and encouraging pupils to use their own familiar linguistic and literary resources to communicate and interpret their own experience. It is a balance between acquiring the specific education required to decode and critically appreciate the literature and performance of theatre in the Western tradition and practising forms of drama which, like the mass-entertainment drama of film and TV, depend on knowledge and experience that is generally available for their enjoyment.

These problems of selection, inclusion and exclusion suggest an approach to curriculum planning in drama that focuses on the core skills and concepts that underpin the diversity of genres, histories and roles within the field of drama. A general foundation course will either prepare pupils for further vocational study in drama or provide them with the skills and knowledge to appreciate the role that drama will continue to play in their lives.

It is not just a question of balance in the curriculum between 'high' and 'low' dramatic practices, but of connection. Rather than reinforcing the socially constructed differences between 'high' and 'low' forms of drama, a new conception of the dramatic curriculum should stress the connections: *the shared processes of production and reception*. There is no reason why dramatic literacy, like verbal literacy, cannot be taught through the vernacular and informal 'texts' and text-making processes that are familiar to, and representative of, the pupils themselves. This is the aim of the structures provided in the *Resources Section* – to teach the full range of dramatic literacy through making dramas that are inclusive of, and responsive to, the lives and maturity levels of 11–14-year-old pupils.

There is one further assumption to be made visible. I want to suggest that a drama curriculum should focus on the live experience of making and responding to theatre and that within this focus the emphasis should be on theatre as a **performance art** rather than on theatre as a branch of literature. In English-speaking countries, pupils will tend to encounter dramatic literature and to develop the codes of interpreting and responding to dramatic literature in English studies or language arts programmes. In many schools, knowledge and understanding of the drama of film and TV may be taught as part of English or as Media Studies. It makes sense, therefore, to concentrate on how theatre is brought to life.

At first sight this assumption – that the drama curriculum should focus on live theatre – appears to be in contradiction to my earlier warnings about the ethnocentricity and social exclusiveness of the Western theatre tradition. What I am suggesting is that the drama curriculum should start from a definition of theatre that is inclusive of a wide range of theatre/drama practices and cultural traditions: a definition that rejects the hierarchisation of these practices into 'high/low', superior/inferior.

I have tried to draw out, from the potential field, certain characteristics that seem to be common to all forms of live theatre and to use these characteristics to offer a definition of theatre that is inclusive but also limited, in order to make some distinction between what is theatre and what is not theatre.

The four conditions of theatre

These conditions are:

1 An elected context	Theatre is by choice. It is bracketed off from 'daily life'. It is a mode of *live* experience that is special and different from our everyday experience. The 'choice' is often formalised by the spatial and temporal separation of theatre from life, so that performances are advertised to occur at a certain time within a designated performance space.
2 Transformation of self, time and place	Within the 'elected context' there is the expectation that a 'virtual present' or 'imagined world', which is representative of an 'absent' or 'other' reality, will be enacted through the symbolic transformation of presence, time and space. The performance space, the experience of time and the actors all become something different for the duration of the performance.
3 Social and aesthetic rules/frame	Theatre is a rule-bound activity. Certain rules are 'perpetual' – there must be a choice as to whether an event is experienced as theatre, for instance. Others are tied to particular paradigms – the rules and conventions of a particular form or period of theatre. These rules relate both to the art of theatre and also to the terms of the social encounter that is theatre; being silent or joining in, for instance.
4 Actor–audience interactions:	There is always a performer function (the transformed self) and an audience function (reacting and responding to the performer's actions). In some forms of theatre these functions are clearly separated – the audience comes to communicate with actors. In others, the separation is less defined – a group come together to communicate as actors and as audience. Whatever form theatre takes, there must be communication between performer and audience.

Because of these four conditions, theatre is the live experience that is shared when people imagine and interact as if they were other than themselves in some other place at another time. Meanings in theatre are created by the actor, for both spectators and other participants, through the fictional and symbolic uses of human presence in time and space. These may be enhanced by the symbolic use of objects, sounds and lights. Theatre is understood through its conventions which are the indicators of the ways in which time, space and presence can interact and be imaginatively shaped to communicate different kinds of meanings.

Local vs National Curriculum

This discussion about the content and parameters of a curriculum for drama is only possible because, at the time of writing, drama is not a formal or National Curriculum subject in many countries. There isn't an agreed and legislative framework for drama as there is for Science or History. If such a framework existed then our discussion might be more concerned with its implementation and methods of delivery within a school. This situation is both a strength and a weakness.

The strength is that, in the absence of a national agreement about a drama curriculum, schools are free to design a curriculum for drama that is particularly responsive to local needs: to the local context for drama provided by a particular school representing a particular community. The local differences between what different communities might value in drama may be considerable. Here are three examples from schools within a five-mile radius of each other.

Drama as personal and social education

In this school many of the pupils have low self-esteem and lack effective social skills for productive and constructive interpersonal relationships. Drama is not offered as an examination subject because the levels of truancy make it near impossible to complete the required practical coursework. In this school, drama is valued for the contribution it makes to the personal, social and moral education of the pupils, as well as for being an immediate and practical forum for creativity. Drama is seen as being essential to the school's efforts to raise the expectations of both the pupils and the community and to develop the interpretative and interpersonal skills needed for the management of a happy and successful life. Understandably, the drama curriculum closely reflects the value and expectation that is placed on it by the school and its community. Its aims and objectives foreground the development and assessment of skills and objectives associated with the Personal, Social and Moral Education (PSME) curriculum.

Drama as English

In the second school, drama at KS3 (11–14) is taught as part of English but it has its own curriculum documentation and status. There are two strands that are emphasised – the personal and social rewards to be gained from the literary study, performance and watching of plays and the contribution that drama can make to the development of literacy. The aims and the objectives for the drama curriculum closely reflect the references to drama in the Statutory Orders for English and the assessment is either related to the national SATs for *Shakespeare* and *Speaking and Listening* or to written work in response to drama.

Drama as subject

The final school in the sample shares many of the social characteristics of the first but it is further into the process of regeneration. In a climate of league tables, performance indicators and local competition for resources the school is keen to boost the numbers of pupils achieving A–C grades in GCSE exams. In recent years, drama pupils have done very well in their exams, and the school supports an increase in the number of pupils choosing drama as an exam option. Drama is taught by specialist teachers and the curriculum at KS3 is seen as a preparation for the GCSE course. There is a strong emphasis on: the development and assessment of individual dramatic skills; the history of theatre, particularly Greek and Elizabethan; the production and presentation of plays by pupils. The aims and objectives for the KS3 curriculum are borrowed from the GCSE syllabus.

The different positions that have been taken in these schools goes beyond pragmatism and survival. They are not cynical responses to feeling marginalised. In all three schools drama is highly valued – but for different reasons. They are all positive attempts to frame a local interpretation of a drama curriculum.

Which brings us to the weakness of the local curriculum. There are two dangers. The first is professional insecurity. In the absence of a nationally agreed framework for drama, an individual drama teacher has no external and objective point of reference for her own curriculum plans. Am I doing the right things? Am I making fair assessments? What are other schools doing? The third school in our sample had used the aims and objectives from their GCSE syllabus for their KS3 curriculum, which is one way of tempering the local with an external validating authority. The second danger is that the local curriculum can be based on a highly idiosyncratic and ideologically motivated selection. What is taught may be left to the whim of an individual teacher and may reflect personal prejudices and interests rather than the breadth and depth of study which is a pupil's entitlement.

The potential strength of a curriculum that is based on a nationally agreed framework is that it provides a very visible and discussible curriculum. It is a public framework which gives pupils and their communities as well as schools a sense of what is expected, what is included and what will be assessed *in every school*. Different communities will respond to the content and ideology of national curriculum planning in different ways but at least a national agreement provides some external, relatively objective and visible material to discuss.

A common subject core: modes of activity

In England, where drama does not enjoy subject status within the National Curriculum, there are a number of national documents of guidance available as well as the specific references to drama in the Programmes of Study for English. In Scotland there are guidelines for drama within the national framework for Expressive Arts.

A close examination of the various sources of national guidance for drama reveals that there is some measure of general agreement that the aims and objectives for drama should reflect the three positions outlined earlier:

- Drama as personal, social and moral education
- Drama as English
- Drama as a subject in its own right.

There is also general agreement that drama, like the other arts, involves three interrelated modes of activity.

Making

This includes all the processes and stages of production used in the creation of a drama event, whether it is a tableau or a full-length presentation. Making implies 'doing' but it also depends on 'knowing'. In other words, the pupil's 'making' is dependent on knowing *how* to make. In this sense, the assessment of pupils' making skills is in part an assessment of how well they have used what they have learnt about the processes of production in drama. Because drama is a social event, the processes of production include the social and the aesthetic: the *social ability* to form effective production groups and to negotiate a dramatic representation that is itself representative of the production group; and the *aesthetic ability* to shape the representation into an appropriate form to communicate the production group's intentions.

The skills and understandings of making, or devising, drama that pupils need to develop might include:

- how to establish objective working relationships with other pupils regardless of gender, ability or personal prejudices;
- how to research, collate and select information needed for the work;
- how to translate a source for drama from page-to-stage: the source might be a playscript, story, poem, documentary text, image or idea;
- how to select and use an appropriate dramatic convention or form for the work;
- how to turn ideas about actions into actions;
- how to help to edit and refine a group's initial attempts at finding actions so that the performed action will stand alone without the need for further explanation or justification from the production group.

Performing

This includes the skills and knowledge needed for the execution of a drama event. Performance implies that there will be a transformation of self, time and space. A virtual 'reality', or 'drama world' will be communicated within the actual context of the classroom, studio or theatre. In the Western tradition of theatre, the assumption is that a performance will be produced for another audience; there tends to be a rigid separation between the producers of the event and those who come to experience it. But performance can also mean a drama event that is shared among a group, who may take it in turns to perform for each other or who may all be simultaneously involved in the performance of a virtual 'reality'.

The skills and understandings of performing that pupils need to develop might include:

- How to transform our daily behaviour and physical presence into 'other' characters, lives, physical presences.
- How to choose a performance style: realism, symbolism, expressionism.

- How to communicate different levels of meaning/interpretation through performance.
- How to work effectively in ensemble performance: acting and reacting, giving and responding to cues.
- How an actor's work can be enhanced by light, sound and objects.
- How spaces can be transformed into 'other places' at 'other times'.

Responding

This includes the skills and knowledge of responding to drama in its written and performed forms. Responding includes articulating subjective responses to drama; making sense of feelings and thoughts aroused by the drama. It also includes the ability to deconstruct the drama using appropriate semiotic and critical codes; explaining how the elements of drama have been used to construct an effective dramatic instance. This process of critical deconstruction requires some objective knowledge of the 'grammar' of theatre and drama and of the histories of such 'grammars'. The skills and understandings of responding to theatre that pupils need to develop might include:

- How read dramatic literature as a potential performance text.
- How to 'physicalise' a character from the clues given in a literary source.
- How to deconstruct a moment of drama in terms of the elements used and its place within a dramatic structure or process.
- How to begin to develop a critical and common language for making our own subjective response to drama public.
- How to create the climate for giving and receiving public feedback on performance.

The three modes of drama – *making, performing, responding* – provide a basis for balance in a school drama curriculum. All three are associated with learning in drama and it is a teacher's responsibility to ensure that pupils engage with drama through each of the three modes. The detailed curricular framework for the activities will, however, still reflect local variations.

A curriculum model for drama at KS3

In this section I will suggest a model of a drama curriculum for KS3. This modelling takes into account:

- the specific purposes that a school might have for drama;
- the need to ensure continuity between KS2 and KS4;
- the influence of the National Strategy with its emphasis on teaching and learning styles, as well as other guidance on effective teaching and learning; and
- the need to include and cover the Drama objectives within the National Strategy.

A curriculum model has three interrelated dimensions: **Curriculum plan** (what is taught and when it is taught within the KS); **Pedagogy** (the teaching approaches that will be used to deliver the curriculum effectively and progressively for all pupils); and **Assessment** (how the curriculum content and pedagogy will be assessed, recorded and reported on). As far as possible, these three dimensions need to be consistent with each other. In other words, the assessment dimension should be consistent with, and tailored to, the specific learning objectives for the key stage and the values and pedagogic practices used to teach the objectives.

Continuity and progression in Key Stages 2–4

KS2

The lack of a national framework for drama, together with the patchy provision of drama in KS1/2 (5–11), make it difficult for teachers in KS3 to know what prior experiences pupils might have had in the subject. Some may have had regular classes in drama in school. Some may have received private classes in drama and dance. Some may (because of social and geographical circumstances) be regular theatre-goers. We have noted that a curriculum for drama should not be based on the assumption that all children have had all or any of these prior experiences. However, it is safe to assume that the majority of pupils coming into KS3:

- will have experienced some form of imaginative and imitative role play in school or in the community;

- will be aware that people behave as social actors who take on roles that are appropriate to social situations;

- will watch, understand and regularly discuss drama on TV, video or film most nights of the week;

- will have some sense of narrative genres, structure and plot development (even if this is no more than a simple beginning, middle and end structure) and an awareness that stories sequence people and events in time and space;

- will have some sense of the conventions of written, improvised and role-taking forms of drama as part of their engagement with the National Literacy Strategy;

- will have some sense of *cultural logic*, in other words, their own socialisation will have taught them something about how people might behave and react in particular circumstances. Children's responses to the question 'What happens next?' often reveal their sense of narrative (this is what usually happens in a story like this), and their sense of cultural logic – 'my existing understanding and observation of human behaviour makes me think that this would happen next'.

KS4

The approved examination syllabi for Drama at GCSE provide teachers at KS4 (14–16) with a planned and nationally agreed curriculum for drama. For this reason, and because all pupils at KS3 are, potentially, working towards the levels of achievement in drama expected at GCSE level, it makes sense to consider the aims and objectives for GCSE within a model KS3 curriculum.

The current GCSE syllabi for drama reveal a general agreement about the broad aims for teaching and learning in drama and theatre at KS4. There are often three common aims to be found, which cover:

1. understanding and using a wide variety of dramatic forms and concepts;
2. being an effective group member in making, performing and responding to drama; and
3. the appreciation and review of live theatre experiences and evaluation of one's own performance and that of others.

Incorporating these common aims of GCSE into the KS3 curriculum provides some measure of external validation and it ensures that there is progression towards KS4. However, we should remember that the majority of pupils who take drama at KS3 are unlikely to choose it as a vocational option for further study in the examination years. The KS3 curriculum has to be for all pupils and it should provide a synoptic conclusion for those who will not experience drama in KS4.

Working with the National Strategy objectives

The Drama objectives within the National Strategy are specifically designed and framed for KS3 and are therefore an important source of guidance for designing a local drama curriculum. These objectives are linked to years, so there is also a suggestion of progression across the key stage.

The Drama objectives are:

Year 7   SL 15: develop drama techniques to explore in role a variety of situations and texts or respond to stimuli;
SL 16: work collaboratively to devise and present scripted and unscripted pieces, which maintain the attention of an audience;
SL 17: extend their spoken repertoire by experimenting with language in different roles and dramatic contexts;
SL 18: develop drama techniques and strategies for anticipating, visualising and problem-solving in different learning contexts;
SL 19: reflect on and evaluate their own presentations and those of others.

Year 8   SL 13: reflect on their participation in drama and identify areas for their development of dramatic techniques, e.g. keep a reflective record of their contributions to dramatic improvisation and presentation;
SL 14: develop the dramatic techniques that enable them to create and sustain a variety of roles;
SL 15: explore and develop ideas, issues and relationships through work in role;
SL 16: collaborate in, and evaluate, the presentation of dramatic performances, scripted and unscripted, which explore character, relationships and issues.

Year 9 SL 11: recognise, evaluate and extend the skills and techniques they have developed through drama;

SL 12: use a range of drama techniques, including work in role, to explore issues, ideas and meanings, e.g. by playing out hypotheses, by changing perspectives;

SL 13: develop and compare different interpretations of scenes or plays by Shakespeare or other dramatists;

SL 14: convey action, character, atmosphere and tension when scripting and performing plays;

SL 15: write critical evaluations of performances they have seen or in which they have participated, identifying the contributions of the writer, director and actors.

The Drama objectives within the National Strategy are limited by their position within the Framework objectives for English. They are a subset within the Speaking and Listening objectives (SLO), which relate to one of the three learning strands in the National Curriculum for English; Reading and Writing being the others. This positioning creates some anomalies which need taking into account when planning a subject-specific and culturally inclusive drama curriculum:

- A drama curriculum will also include subject-specific reading and writing objectives in addition to speaking and listening. Learning how to read and use texts from a dramatic perspective. Writing in a variety of forms for a variety of purposes including scripts, diaries and records of experience in drama.

- The SLOs assume that drama will be taught as part of English and this shapes the selection of what is included and excluded from the potential field of drama. In particular, the SLOs do not give sufficient value to visual, physical and technical learning in drama. The focus on objectives which are closely related to the English curriculum also means that in themselves the SLOs might not give a sufficient foundation for further study and experience of drama in later key stages.

- The SLOs do not give the kind of priority to the rich variety of personal, social and community development objectives which are valued by many drama teachers and their school communities.

A curriculum plan for KS3

With these considerations in mind, I have framed a curriculum plan below which is based on the idea of a locally defined curriculum which reflects and includes the National Strategy objectives, the common aims for GCSE and potential prior learning at KS2, as well as a clear sense of a curriculum which has bold personal and social objectives for learning in drama. The plan is built around three Specialist Learning Strands, framed around three principal roles in theatre making – Actor, Director and Critic: Acting/Interacting; Directing/Managing; Reviewing/Evaluating. These three Specialist Learning Strands seek to encompass and mesh together key subject-specific and transferable artistic and social skills and understandings. The principle is that as pupils develop their skills and competences in the artistic roles of actor, director and critic they are also developing their social roles and capacity to be social actors, managers of team-based creative project work and effective and critical evaluators of their own work and that of others.

Acting is the key role in both artistic and social development. In many forms of KS3 drama, nothing happens until a pupil or group of pupils indicate their willingness to take part and begin to make things happen. For many pupils this is a highly challenging moment, which needs self-confidence and a lack of self-consciousness. The teacher's role is to encourage and protect, through contracting, all pupils so that they can find the confidence and self-esteem needed to take action in the drama classroom.

I want pupils to understand that the same is true in the social world. In other words, change will only happen if individuals and groups of people are prepared to take action and make it happen. An effective social actor – someone who is prepared to stand up for themselves and others and to take action – must also overcome the same problems of self-confidence and self-consciousness as an artistic actor.

Acting	Interacting
Acting is at the heart of drama. Drama invites pupils to 'imagine themselves differently' in a wide variety of roles and situations for a range of educational purposes. During KS3, pupils will develop their skills as role players and also begin to learn the skills of characterisation and the rehearsed performance of character to an audience.	Drama is a social art form. Learning to work and interact sensitively and effectively with others is important to the creation of 'ensemble' acting and to the collective realisation of ideas in drama. Working on developing the skills needed for effective classroom interactions in drama is intended to transfer into other learning/working situations the pupils meet.
Directing	**Managing**
Learning the skills and understandings needed to shape ideas into a communicable dramatic statement will become a key feature of drama at KS3. Directing includes becoming skilful at using, arranging and designing the elements of drama. It also includes developing historical and formal knowledge of styles, genres etc.	Being given opportunities to 'direct' group work goes hand-in-hand with developing the skills of managing and taking responsibility for the effective and inclusive management of groups and the delivery of teamwork. In order to direct effectively, pupils must also be able to sensitively and publicly manage time, resources, problems and deadlines.
Reviewing	**Evaluating**
Developing the ability to critically and appropriately reflect on and review their own and others' performances and performances they have seen. Critical reviewing requires appropriate knowledge of the different choices available in the production and performance of drama as well as some historical and comparative cultural knowledge of styles, genres of performance and text.	Evaluating includes: learning how to self- and peer-evaluate progress and set appropriate targets; developing critical thinking skills and becoming more conscious of self and others; reflecting on the personal and social significance of the work.

In the curriculum plan on pp. 14–15, each of the Specialist Learning Strands has its own key specialist objectives. These specialist objectives are cross-referenced to appropriate KS3 Strategy objectives for each year from the *Drama Objectives Bank*, in order to give a sense of progression across the Key Stage and to ensure that the specialist objectives include and cover the statutory orders for drama in the National Curriculum and the KS3 Strategy guidance.

Matching teaching approaches to the curriculum plan

The *Drama Objectives Bank* includes the following statement:

> Teaching needs to be based around objectives and draw on a repertoire of conventions and techniques in relation to a text or situation. It is not enough for teachers to arrange situations and trust that this will encourage pupils to develop their skills in drama. Pupils need focussed and effective teaching to enable them to develop through encountering, investigating, experimenting with and reflecting on a wide range of drama experiences.

High-quality and authentic learning opportunities are, of course, dependent on the skilful and selective use of high-quality teaching approaches. Through our teaching we breathe life into the curriculum plan and seek to make it accessible, possible and relevant to the full ability range within a class.

A pedagogic contract for KS3 drama

The roles, skills and knowledge needed for effective drama teaching are given detailed attention in Section Two of this book. One of the key skills discussed there is contracting ground rules with pupils to ensure that they use the space safely and feel safe enough with the teacher and others to fully engage in drama. The explicit discussion of rules and boundaries with the class should also include discussing and negotiating a pedagogic contract, which will make the teacher's pedagogic principles clear and transparent for the class.

The pedagogic contract described below is an umbrella or frame for determining the specific teaching approaches needed to deliver the objectives in the curriculum plan. It is a statement of general intentions or orientations towards the teaching and learning partnership in the drama classroom.

This pedagogic contract is based on the idea of trying to achieve balance between:

Mindfulness ←——————→ Playfulness

Mindfulness	Playfulness
■ We think about what we do	■ We feel safe to experiment, risk, fail, bend and stretch the rules
■ We take the human content and context of our work seriously	■ We play with language and other sign-systems to find the new, the unspoken, the fresh voice
■ We consider how what we learn might change us and who we are becoming	■ We are creative in the world
■ We are mindful of self, others and the world	■ Nothing is 'sacred'!

Classroom Management

(continued on p. 16)

A curriculum plan for KS3 drama

Specialist Learning Strand objectives		National Strategy Year 7 objectives	National Strategy Year 8 objectives	National Strategy Year 9 objectives
Acting A1: use and control the elements of drama, particularly voice and the body in space A2: use voice, gesture and movement to convey meaning to an audience, making disciplined use of the conventions of performance A3: make effective use of space and relationships with other actors A4: play a wide range of characters in different styles based on research, observation and personal interpretation	**Interacting** IA1: work as part of an ensemble – acting and reacting to others IA2: speak with confidence in front of the class when explaining and presenting IA3: observe and actively maintain social rules for class discussion IA4: contribute ideas and establish productive working relationships with other group members through: discussion, attentive listening and accepting feedback from others	SL 15: develop drama techniques to explore in role a variety of situations and texts or respond to stimuli SL 16: work collaboratively to devise and present scripted and unscripted pieces, which maintain the attention of an audience SL 17: extend their spoken repertoire by experimenting with language in different roles and dramatic contexts	SL 14: develop the dramatic techniques that enable them to create and sustain a variety of roles SL 15: explore and develop ideas, issues and relationships through work in role	SL 11: recognise, evaluate and extend the skills and techniques they have developed through drama
Directing D1: make creative and symbolic use of the elements of drama – time, space, presence, light, sound and objects – from own experience of drama and from watching drama D2: recognise and name the conventions and techniques used in drama and something of their history, e.g. monologue, tableau, role-play D3: understand the different contributions that actors, audi-	**Managing** M1: learn to negotiate with others in a group and adapt to and accommodate other people's ideas M2: propose tasks, goals or actions to move group work on M3: ask for and act on information, opinions, feelings and ideas from others M4: suggest ways of synthesising and integrating ideas offered in groups M5: manage time and other	SL 18: develop drama techniques and strategies for anticipating, visualising and problem-solving in different learning contexts	SL 13: reflect on participation in drama and identify areas for development of dramatic techniques, e.g. *keep a reflective record of contributions to dramatic improvisation and presentation*	SL 12: use a range of drama techniques, including work in role, to explore issues, ideas and meanings, e.g. *by playing out hypotheses, by changing perspectives* SL13: develop and compare different interpretations of scenes or plays by Shakespeare or other dramatists SL 14: convey action, character, atmosphere and tension when scripting and performing plays

			SL 15: write critical evaluations of performances seen or participated in, identifying the contributions of the writer, director and actors
			SL 16: collaborate in, and evaluate, the presentation of dramatic performances, scripted and unscripted, which explore character, relationships and issues
		SL 19: reflect on and evaluate own presentations and those of others	
ences, directors, writers, designers and technicians make to a dramatic event D4: direct the work of writers, actors and designers into a coherent dramatic statement D5: translate initial ideas and responses into drama, which might include a tableau, an improvisation or a script D6: recognise different ways of structuring and organising plays **Reviewing** R1: identify historical and current genres of drama, e.g. tragedy, comedy, mime, mask, physical, soap opera R2: use a critical and specialist vocabulary for discussing drama, e.g. gesture, symbol, tension, rhythm and pace, contrast etc R3: write reviews of drama that accurately refer to what was seen, heard and experienced during the drama R4: use specialist vocabulary confidently and sustain discussion on a text R5: evaluate and analyse the structure, meaning and impact of plays studied, watched or taken part in	resources responsibly and appropriately M6: lead and take responsibility for completing group tasks **Evaluating** E1: identify and evaluate the different choices that can be made in drama that lead groups to make different interpretations/representations of the same material E2: develop their critical thinking about texts, issues and situations through work in role. Analyse and account for their responses to texts E3: evaluate their own progress and set personal targets for development		

Planned ← → **Lived**

Planned	Lived
■ Our local communities have a clear plan or map of where we are going, what we need to learn, how we will be valued	■ We are human, with human needs, emotions, fears and dreams
■ We are entitled to the knowledge that will give us power	■ Our experiences shape our worlds, our learning and our 'becoming'
	■ Our differences are our strength

Necessary constraint ← → **Necessary freedom**

Necessary constraint	Necessary freedom
■ We work within a community and live within its traditions, codes and rules	■ We are individuals
■ We access and work with culturally powerful genres of communication	■ We must have choices in our learning
■ We have structure and structures to grow with	■ We are free to change our worlds
	■ Knowing the 'rules' gives us more choices, greater freedom to be

Imagination ← → **Knowledge**

Imagination	Knowledge
■ We imagine what we cannot yet know	■ What we imagine is anchored to what we know
■ We imagine and re-imagine ourselves and others	■ We realise that what we think we know is often 'imaginary' (cultural)
■ We are free from ideologies that replace the imagination	■ We create our own 'map of the world'
■ Imagining reminds us that we are human	■ We are changeable and so is the world

The use of a pedagogic contract such as this, which is openly discussed and modified with the class, is a means of establishing an appropriate climate for teaching and learning which is not necessarily subject-specific. It underpins the importance of pupils being involved in and aware of the values and principles of high-quality and authentic pedagogy. It might, for instance, be useful to remind the class of the need to keep an appropriate balance between *mindfulness* and *playfulness*! Too mindful and the work will become dull and uninspiring; too playful and nothing gets done or learnt.

The pedagogic contract will guide the selection of specific teaching approaches, which are of particular relevance to the Specialist Learning Strand objectives of the curriculum plan. In other words, in addition to the pedagogic contract, teachers also need to clearly identify the appropriate teaching and learning strategies for the objectives in the curriculum plan.

Selecting appropriate teaching approaches for an objective

The *Drama Objectives Bank* provides detailed guidance on appropriate teaching approaches for each of the drama objectives in the National Strategy. In the table on pp. 17–19 I have selected and rearranged the guidance to match my own local curriculum model based on the three learning strands that I have outlined (see p. 11).

Selected teaching approaches for the Specialist Learning Strands

Acting	Interacting
■ Demonstrate and then provide opportunities for pupils to take on roles, particularly adult roles that require them to imagine themselves differently ■ Model how to identify each role's or character's 'given circumstances' based on clues in the text or through discussion of the situation being dramatised ■ Teach pupils how to represent characters in context in 'here and now' situations, using visual, aural, linguistic, spatial and physical signs to convey a 'living reality' for an audience ■ Model ways of communicating character through a range of techniques, including *teacher-in-role; tableaux; hot seating* ■ Use a variety of techniques and conventions to explore character, settings and plot through drama rather than through discussion ■ Encourage and reward pupils' responses which are experimental and non-realist in terms of the use of body and voice ■ Show pupils how to receive and interpret comments constructively rather than defensively and how to seek clarification from commentators ■ Show pupils that their work in role can develop their critical thinking through exploring a text or situation. What they say and do is determined by who they are in the drama and the demands of the situation that they face	■ Establish effective working environments that encourage pupils to contribute ideas and responses and to comment sensitively and appropriately on each other's ideas and contributions ■ Establish, explain and model the ground rules for collaborative working and the conventions for presentation ■ Encourage pupils to feel confident to express ideas which are alternative to or different from those expressed by the majority in the group ■ Plan opportunities for pupils to experience and use powerful registers of language ■ Encourage less confident pupils to take on powerful roles in the drama, and create situations where pupils need to solve problems through appropriate dialects and registers ■ Ensure that pupils respond to each other's work at various stages of development, using the appropriate tone and terminology ■ Create a protective environment for pupils to experiment with their voices and movement without self-consciousness ■ Provide opportunities for pupils to interact with others in role, both in improvisation and by adding *thought-tracking; soundscaping; and hot-seating* to another pupil's or group's work

Directing	Managing
<ul><li>Introduce a wide range of dramatic conventions related to work in role and explain their purposes and effectiveness</li><li>Model the creation of pieces of drama from different stimuli</li><li>Direct examples of group work to demonstrate how to communicate ideas to an audience through dramatic techniques and conventions of staging</li><li>Teach pupils about the different roles involved in a production and how they relate to each other</li><li>Demonstrate and explore how lighting, props and staging can enhance the dramatic communication and realisation of ideas</li><li>Identify and use examples of good work as models for other groups to follow</li><li>Compare different dramatic interpretations of a scene so that pupils become aware of the variety of possibilities</li><li>Use brief extracts from plays to demonstrate how what characters say can be juxtaposed with visual and aural images to create new meanings</li><li>Model different possibilities for action and use of space suggested by a script</li></ul>	<ul><li>Model ways of negotiating a consensus of ideas and conflict resolution strategies</li><li>Make explicit use of targets related to achievement and specify the criteria that will be used for assessment</li><li>Challenge pupils to take responsibility for a dramatic idea by suggesting that they lead others in the exploration</li><li>Model activities which challenge the pupils and demand co-operation and negotiation in paired and small-group work</li><li>Demonstrate how to identify, negotiate and agree targets and criteria for self/peer assessment of group work</li><li>Allocate specific responsibilities for group work including, where appropriate, actors, designers, directors, chairing discussion, time-keeping</li><li>Model skills necessary for effective management of a group project</li></ul>

Reviewing	Evaluating
■ Ensure that time is planned for appropriate reflection on both the form and content of pupils' work ■ Establish a common language and subject-specific vocabulary by teaching, using and reinforcing key terms. Use word walls to record and embed the vocabulary and sentence structure required for a particular register ■ Introduce and model the use of subject-specific language for critical exploration and evaluation in speech and writing ■ Promote the use of reflective journals and feature them in shared reading and writing. Guide pupils to use them in a variety of ways, including writing in role, communal writing, planning suggestions, decision-making, critical appraisal and analysis of issues and meaning ■ Explore examples via shared reading of pupils' comments on drama they have seen or taken part in ■ Ask pupils to make brief notes on a performance, supported by writing frames when necessary, to summarise the story, suggest what the major theme is and give reasons for which characters were the most interesting	■ Establish talk as the core medium for learning in drama and ensure that pupils are given every opportunity to discuss, explore and negotiate through talk ■ Create opportunities for critical reflection so that pupils think about and articulate their insights from the drama experience ■ Ensure that lessons have reflection and evaluation as learning objectives from the outset ■ Provide pupils with the means of making visual explorations and presentations of ideas, including OHPs, digital imagery and Power Point as well as art-making materials ■ Encourage the use of mini-plenaries within the lesson to provide opportunities for formative reflection ■ Use *role-on-the-wall* to identify, record and develop what is known about characters from text or exploration

Structuring lessons effectively, based on the objectives and teaching approaches

Structuring learning experiences through drama is a key teaching skill, which is given detailed attention in Section Two. The *Drama Objectives Bank* provides a useful model for the basic structure of a lesson plan or scheme of work, which is consistent with the emphasis on high-quality teaching and learning in the National Strategy. This suggested model reflects the four dimensions of authentic pedagogy, which have emerged from international research. The four dimensions are:

Intellectual quality: having high expectations of the effort that pupils can make and what they can achieve through appropriate teaching and learning strategies.

Relevance: ensuring that teaching approaches establish relevance for learners in terms of their own lives or with real world problems and issues.

Social support: establishing a productive, well-managed and safe learning environment which is inclusive of the diversity of needs within the learning group.

Recognition of difference: ensuring that teaching approaches and materials are inclusive of a diverse range of cultural and ethnic identities.

Locate the lesson or sequence of lessons in the context of:
- the scheme of work
- pupils' prior knowledge
- pupils' preferred learning styles

Identify clearly the essential objective(s) for pupils in terms of:
- their knowledge, understanding, attitude and skills
- their attitudes and personal development

Structure the lesson as a series of episodes by:
- separating the learning into distinct stages or steps

Decide how to teach each episode, then choose:
- the best pedagogic approach
- the most appropriate teaching and learning strategies
- the most effective organisation for each episode

Ensure coherence by providing:
- a stimulating start to the lesson
- transition between episodes which recapitulate and launch new episodes
- a final plenary that reviews learning

Structuring lessons which are progressively challenging

One purpose of the curriculum model is to ensure that in terms of the three parts of the model – plan; pedagogy; assessment – there is a clear sense of progression from pupils' prior knowledge of drama at KS2 towards the demands of the KS4 curriculum. In this sense, progression is the motor that drives the curriculum model suggested here.

Since the first edition of this book there has been considerable attention paid to trying to define and describe how pupils 'get better at doing drama'. In many schools, drama teachers are encouraged to specify levels of achievement for individual pupils, in common with National Curriculum subjects. The *Drama Objectives Bank* takes a different approach, which is to suggest performance indicators for each of the objectives to help teachers to assess whether classes or individuals demonstrate the performance indicator always, sometimes or rarely, with the suggestion that progression is evidenced by the frequency with which learning behaviours and outcomes match the selected indicators. I have adopted this simpler approach to assessing progression in the assessment framework that follows.

Three key principles of progression in the curriculum model

Here I want to focus on ensuring that the curriculum plan and teaching approaches are also based on a sense of progression across the key stage. In general terms, there are three key principles of progression to be borne in mind when planning lessons and sequences of lessons.

1. **Pupils should take responsibility for making *informed* choices about the form and direction of their work.**

    But the ability to make informed choices is dependent on and limited by:
    - knowledge and experience of 'form' and the histories/traditions of 'form'; knowing what the 'choices' are;
    - the skills needed to articulate and negotiate ideas with others in and out of the artistic process; and
    - knowledge and experience in matching 'means' and 'meanings'; recognising that form creates content, content suggests form. You can't take responsibility unless you have been given responsibility.

2. **Pupils should become increasingly selective and complex in their use of 'sign' and gesture to make and represent meanings.**

    But this ability is dependent on the degree of explicit attention that the curriculum has given to:
    - *reflexiveness* – drawing attention to 'theatre-as-theatre' rather than as an 'illusionary experience'; the 'nuts-and-bolts' of theatre production – how the elements and conventions of drama are being used – are made visible to pupils;
    - *dramaturgy* – drawing attention to the 'weave' of the actions in a drama event; pupils regularly analyse how moments of effective drama are constructed or choreographed; and
    - *modelling* – providing live experience and analysis of theatre artists working in a variety of forms and traditions.

3. **Pupils should be assessed on what they *make* rather than on what they claim, or are imagined, to experience.**

    But in KS3 there should be an increasing emphasis on pupils being able to make drama as well as to experience teacher-led structures.

In the mainstream tradition, writings and other forms of commentary on theatre tend to focus on psychological questions in the work: how a performance reveals the private and social psychology of character; how the actor must work on understanding and revealing the psychology of a character; how an audience is psychologically affected by performance. Despite this emphasis, we shouldn't base our assessments on what we imagine to be the private psychological states of the pupils – their 'belief' and 'depth of feeling' for example. What is assessable is either what we see and hear them do in their drama work, or some account or analysis of their experience that can also be seen or heard by others.

Progression in theatre-making

In order to ensure that these key principles of progression can operate in practice, the curriculum model needs to provide an increasing challenge to the pupils' ability to make, perform and respond to drama. The curriculum model can be seen as a form of 'scaffolding' which, through a carefully wrought frame of steps and stages, allows pupils to build on their existing and prior experiences and knowledge of drama towards the experience and knowledge that they will either need for further study or for a terminal point in their school-based drama experience.

In the table below, I have suggested certain progressions that a drama curriculum might develop. The categories respond to a pedagogic progression from the simple unreflexive realism of younger pupils' drama-making, in which the teacher is very much at the centre of a class's work, towards pupils being given and taking increasing responsibility for their own group work, with the teacher working in the margins, guiding, managing, monitoring and assessing the work of groups.

The categories also reflect a certain aesthetic progression, or directions, in the development of twentieth-century Western theatre. These directions are characteristic of the *avant-garde* line of Meyerhold, Brecht, Grotowski and Boal and other practitioners, who pioneered different post-naturalist theatre movements – symbolism, expressionism, physical, and social expressionism – to challenge the dominance of realism and naturalism in the conventional theatre.

Once again, it is important to stress that the progression is not hierarchical: it is historical. The forms of drama that younger pupils enjoy and the forms of theatre that they draw on will continue to play an important role in their drama work and leisure.

From (KS2)	Progression (KS3)	To (KS4)
rules	<u>from</u> simple structures based on the rules of game, or taking turns, or pursuing simple objectives: arguing, persuading, describing events <u>towards</u> language and behaviour determined by the frame; the given circumstances of the situation that is being dramatised. Structures that require pupils to communicate the relationship between text (actions) and context (situation)	**frame/*given circumstances***

sign	from	symbol/*Gestus*

recognising and using conventional, or stock, signs to convey mood,
purpose or response, e.g. hanging head to express disappointment, clenching
fists to express frustration or anger. These kinds of conventional sign mean
that same whoever is signing

towards

more subtle and resonant use of gesture; signs that are expressive of, and
particular to, a character or situation, or theme in the drama

---

type	from	**character**

making and taking roles based on cultural or occupational types or collective
identities, i.e. villager, worker, parent, soldier.
How would the villagers respond?

towards

Playing characters with particular social, historical, physical and
psychological 'characteristics' that the pupil either creates or interprets.
How would *this* villager respond?

---

linear narrative	from	**montage**

story drama structures based on a simple sequence of events acted
out naturalistically. The focus is on cause-and-effect and narrative logic

towards

complex episodic structures where the sequence is organised thematically
rather than temporally. The order of episodes is designed to deepen response
to the 'meaning' of events or the 'sub-text' and may use symbolic and
expressive conventions, e.g. alter-ego, dance, mask, tableau

---

illusionary	from	**reflexive**

The 'realism' of 'living through' imagined experiences as if they were
actually occurring; where the emphasis is on creating 'authenticity' or 'reality'

towards

a greater emphasis on *how* drama is made and *what* it is made of. The 'illusion' is
broken and there is a greater emphasis on the shaping and presentation
of work which shows the pupils' control and use of the elements of drama

teacher-centred (whole group)	from	**autonomous dramaturges (small group)**

work that is initiated and led by the teacher who often works: within
the drama (as fellow actor) with the whole class in role; to model register
and role; to create tension for the pupils; to challenge and support pupils

towards

work that is devised in small groups in response to 'tasks' set by the teacher
or decided on by groups. Pupils are expected to make creative decisions
about how best to execute the work.

Assessment in the KS3 curriculum model

How, what and by which means do we assess drama? Any assessment should provide a fair, reliable and objective means of placing a pupil's progress in drama. But there are pragmatic and philosophical issues to be resolved.

Pragmatic issues

The frequency, rigour and detail of assessment in drama will vary according to a number of local factors, some of which we have already discussed. As we have already noted, at a local level schools value drama for different reasons and this valuing will reveal itself in the assessment arrangements. In some schools, assessment may focus on the personal and inter-personal behaviours of pupils. In others the assessment of drama may be subsumed into the assessment of English: the contribution that drama makes to the development of linguistic and literary skills and knowledge. In schools that view KS3 drama as a foundation and recruiting ground for KS4, assessment might focus on pupils' preparedness for further studies in drama leading to a qualification.

The demands for accountability in drama may also vary from school to school, according to the value that drama is given in the curriculum: some schools may require and take note of detailed assessments in drama; in others there may be little point in providing any detail beyond an assessment of a pupil's level of confidence and willingness to work with others in an effective way.

The time given to drama will also be subject to local variations. Pupils who study drama in 35-minute lessons during KS3 cannot be expected to achieve the same standards, or depth and breadth of study, as those who have one-hour lessons. Teachers who are trying to provide meaningful experiences of drama in very short time periods may also be reluctant to spend precious time on the detailed individual assessment of pupils.

Access to resources will also affect pupils' opportunities to develop their abilities to the standards set. In many schools, pupils have limited access to all the elements of drama. Use of space is, for instance, a key skill in all drama work; but it is difficult to develop this skill in the limited space of a classroom, cloakroom or cupboard in which some teachers are forced to teach drama. Similarly, the technical ability to use contrasts of light and sound will depend on access to technology in a school.

There are also considerable problems related to the assessment of individuals in what is an essentially social and ephemeral activity. The problems are of visibility and evidence of individual achievement. Drama teachers, particularly at KS3, tend to have a relationship with groups rather than individuals. In the English classroom, pupils are often engaged in private work even if it is done in social circumstances. The nature of teaching and learning in English allows the teacher to spend time in one-to-one contacts with pupils. Assessment tasks in English tend to be undertaken individually and provide a permanent archive of evidence of a pupil's development. Drama teachers, on the other hand,

- see groups for shorter periods;
- set goals for groups, rather than individuals, to work on;

- work towards group or whole-class presentations that are not permanently recorded; and
- if teaching drama to a whole-year group, find it very difficult to keep track of every pupil.

Philosophical issues

In addition to the practical problems of assessment, there are also philosophical issues that relate to the purposes of drama work and the assessment of 'creativity'.

Drama teachers are responsible for developing and balancing two different aesthetic traditions: the literary and private; and the oral and communal. In the literary and private aesthetic, associated with the restricted art of theatre, there are specific skills associated with the production and reception of theatre that will reveal individual strengths and weaknesses. We comment on the relative skills of different actors; for instance, we audition actors and select them on the basis of their individual skill-levels. At an amateur level, groups and individuals often take part in competitions or graded tests to establish levels of individual achievement. The ability to decode dramatic literature and to produce a written review of performances also requires individual skills that some pupils will possess to a greater extent than others.

In the oral and communal aesthetic, associated with popular forms of entertainment and community art-making, the emphasis tends to be on the quality of the social experience and what is produced collectively rather than on the quality of individual skills and contributions. In the oral and communal tradition, individual differences are masked by the social effects of a group who pool their strengths in order to work towards communal goals. In a real sense, the willingness to take part, regardless of individual ability, is seen as being more important than demonstrating who is the most artistically skilled in the group.

In this sense, much of the drama work that is done in KS3 will serve the same purposes as other communal art – community singing, dancing, storytelling, and ritual. In these community circumstances, we often tend to evaluate the live experience that we share and the communal pleasure of the event rather than the skills of those involved. If I go, as audience, to see a professional dance company, I expect my pleasure to come from the skills of the dancers. If I go clubbing, I want to have a good night out dancing with others – I don't want any feedback on my dance skills, or comment on my physical shape and grace.

In an assessment programme that focuses too strongly on differentiating between pupils on the basis of their individual abilities as performers and respondents in drama, there is a danger of alienating and disempowering those who have neither the restricted skills, nor the inclination to develop them, but who, none the less, derive enormous social and aesthetic benefits from participating in drama.

In a programme that ignores the development and assessment of individual skills, those pupils who have a vocational interest in drama are denied the teaching and assessment they need to develop their individual performer skills. There is a further danger that, in some schools, the reluctance to make individual and visible assessments will be taken as a sign that drama is not a legitimate subject for academic study and reward.

In modern Western societies there is still a belief that 'artists' are specially inspired people who have exceptional 'natural' gifts and whose 'creativity' is also a rare and mysterious quality. This belief leads to a reluctance to make subjective assessments of the 'quality' of pupils' artwork, or to subject their attempts at 'self-expression' to external judgement. Increasingly, however, we are becoming aware that artists are often specially trained rather than specially gifted and that this special training is often made more available to pupils from certain social groups. It is only in the last fifty years or so, that we have seen professional actors who are neither middle class nor European in their origins (although actors often enjoyed the same social status as tinkers prior to the nineteenth century). We are also aware that we all 'create' and exchange our worlds through acts of perception and communication.

The arts are, in this sense, no more than and no less than specialised forms of communication which draw on many of the same skills required in any other form of communication, that is, the ability to communicate experience, which is based on a particular perception of the world, to others in a way that allows them to share and respond to that experience as if it was their own. In this sense, drama is a form of communication in which meanings are shared through the means of dramatic conventions.

Some pupils will communicate more effectively through drama than through other means, just as some will demonstrate a particular aptitude for the sciences or for sport. But, just as with written forms of communication, all pupils require training and instruction in how to use the formal means of communication in drama if they are to achieve their potential. And this training can be assessed objectively, just as it is in written forms of communication.

Assessment based on the *Drama Objectives Bank* guidance

The *Drama Objectives Bank* reminds us that 'Assessment should be a planned part of every lesson, and self-assessment should be part of every pupil's normal pattern of working in drama'. There is detailed guidance on how to assess each of the objectives in the bank, together with a list of possible performance indicators to guide assessment. Below I have selected and reorganised these performance indicators to match the three learning strands in the model curriculum and to suggest potential progression across the key stage. In order for the curriculum model to be effective, there needs to be consistency and coherence between:

The key objective(s) for the lesson

▼

Selected teaching approaches

▼

Assessment opportunities and strategies

▼

Appropriate performance indicators

The key objective(s) for the lesson For instance if in a Year 7, Term 1 sequence of lessons the Specialist Learning Strand key objectives are:

A1: use and control the elements of drama, particularly voice and the body in space

IA1: work as part of an ensemble – acting and reacting to others then, in addition to planning materials and tasks for the sequence of lessons I might use the following **selected teaching approaches** as being particularly appropriate to delivering the key objectives:

- Teach pupils how to represent characters in context in 'here and now' situations, using visual, aural, linguistic, spatial and physical signs to convey a 'living reality' for an audience;

- Model how to identify each role's or character's 'given circumstances' based on clues in the text or through discussion of the situation being dramatised;

- Provide opportunities for pupils to interact with others in role both in improvisation and by adding thought-tracking, soundscaping, hot-seating to another pupil's or group's work.

Assessment opportunities and strategies Planned assessment opportunities and strategies designed to be consistent with the key objectives and selected teaching approaches might include:

- Pupils taking on roles from the text used as a stimulus and being questioned about their motives and circumstances by other pupils, either as themselves or in a given role.

- Individually, or in groups, pupils use, at different stages in the lesson, *role-on-the-wall* to list characteristics and circumstances of their role or character, based on suggestions and clues in the stimulus and the outcomes of their exploratory work in role.

- Groups are asked to make a *tableau* which physically represents the tensions and proxemics in the network of relationships between key characters at a chosen moment in the 'play'; e.g. Juliet's relationships with other characters at the end of Act 1 Sc 5.

Appropriate performance indicators This pattern of key objectives, teaching approaches, assessment opportunities and strategies might suggest looking for evidence of the following Year 7 performance indicators. The pupil:

1. works effectively and co-operatively with others both in an out of role
2. uses voice and movement to convey character, matching dialect and register to role and situation
3. contributes ideas to discussion, listening to and incorporating the ideas of others
4. analyses dialogue in scripts and other texts and forms ideas about characters
5. observes and maintains social rules for class discussion and group work
6. recognises and comments on the dramatic potential of the given circumstances

In this example, the first five selected performance indicators are taken from the Acting/Interacting Learning Strand, and the sixth from the Directing/Managing strand, even though the key objectives belong to the first strand. This is because the indicator is appropriate to the selected acting objectives and because the learning strands themselves are fluid and flexible and I need to be aware of opportunities for learning across the specialist strands.

Assessment based on key performance indicators

L/S	Key Performance Indicators: Yr 7	Key Performance Indicators: Yr 8	Key Performance Indicators: Yr 9
Acting Interacting Always = A Sometimes = S Rarely = R	works effectively and co-operatively with others both in and out of role	uses self-evaluation to set personal targets for improvement	initiates, explores and experiments with new ideas and ways of making, responding to texts/stimuli with imagination and creativity
	uses voice and movement to convey character matching dialect and register to role and situation	can adapt voice and movement to reflect changes in the character's given circumstances	performs in a range of styles and genres conveying different emotions and effects
	contributes ideas to discussion, listening to and incorporating the ideas of others	understands the importance of responding to others' ideas critically but sensitively	interprets stimulus material imaginatively and sensitively using a range of dramatic techniques to explore and develop character
	analyses dialogue in scripts and other texts and forms ideas about characters	works in role in a sustained way to explore issues, ideas and relationships	uses voice and movement to create and portray characters that maintain an audience's interest
	observes and maintains social rules for class discussion and group work	recognises and discusses cultural, moral and social issues raised by characterisation and explorations in role	bases characterisation on research into theme and content
Directing Managing	recognises and comments on the dramatic potential of the given circumstances	identifies issues in the work and finds ways to focus the group on exploration	understands the contribution of technical and design elements and makes appropriate use of them
	structures scenes so that they are coherent to an audience	understands and uses a range of dramatic techniques	works constructively with others to shape performances that offer new insights into issues and ideas
	identifies and uses a wide range of dramatic techniques for exploring, rehearsing and performing	understands the written conventions of a dramatic script and different ways in which plays are structured	can take director's role and discuss, demonstrate and annotate a text to show an interpretation
	uses critical questioning to develop and refine ideas	works collaboratively and in a leadership role to plan and shape dramatic presentations	can explain how costume, setting and technical effects may change audience response, mood and atmosphere
	uses visual, aural and kinaesthetic techniques when problem-solving through drama	reflects on the impact of a performance on an audience and how to modify/improve it	understands how tension is built through performance technique and structure of narrative
	listens to and seeks to integrate ideas which are different from own	uses appropriate registers for analysing, comparing and articulating insights and understandings	
	sets targets and monitors own and peer progress		

L/S	Key Performance Indicators: Yr 7	Key Performance Indicators: Yr 8	Key Performance Indicators: Yr 9
Reviewing Evaluating	keeps basic records of work in a variety of visual and written forms	can give reasons for choices of techniques and other structuring devices	understands and makes appropriate use of subject-specific vocabulary to describe and evaluate texts explored and dramas created
	comments positively and critically on own work and that of others	comments on the effectiveness of dramatic presentations	records personal and critical responses in a variety of ways and sets achievable targets
	recognises and can discuss relationships between form, content and intention in scripts, texts and dramas created	reflects on and discusses the personal and/or social relevance of ideas, issues and relationships explored in the drama	is aware of the way texts are mediated and offers particular perspectives (voice)
	reflects during devising, rehearsal and discussion on relevant themes, ideas and issues	uses appropriate technical terms to write critical evaluations of performances seen or created	recognises and explains how historical/social and changing performance contexts effect the interpretation of texts
	understands and uses appropriate criteria to assess work and inform future planning		structures reviews to inform and engage reader using subject-specific terms to describe elements of performance seen or made
			balances subjective responses with critical evaluations of techniques used by writers, directors, designers and performers

The means of assessment

If assessment is to be used as the basis for establishing levels of ability and discussing development, then it must be permanent, visible and discussible. There has to be some lasting record of achievement that can be referred to by teachers, pupils and parents. It must be visible in the sense that all parties can see, hear or read the same material rather than consider accounts of pupil practice that do not reveal the evidence that is used. It must create the possibility of dialogue about the fairness of the assessment and the negotiation of future goals and targets for improvement. The means of assessment must also be fit for the purpose. There is, as we have noted, a diverse range of skills and activities in drama which may require different instruments for their assessment.

Here I describe some of the commonly used means of assessment in drama:

Instrument	Description
Journals and diaries	Notebooks or folders kept by pupils that contain a record of their responses and working processes during the drama. These may be informal and based on written pupil–teacher dialogues, or structured so that specific tasks, i.e. a character description, are set.
Writing and scripting	Scripted dialogues and/or scenes that might be originals, interpretations or dramatisations from other sources, including improvisation. Assessment is tied to the realisation of particular dramatic intentions or conventions. Writing that emerges from drama – letters, diaries, petitions, instructions, dispositions, etc.
Video and sound records	Video or oral record of class work taken by the teacher or pupil that is a permanent record of a pupil's level of ability at a chosen moment.
Written and standardised tests	Formal tests of pupils' knowledge of texts, genres, history. National standardised tests such as the Shakespeare and Speaking and Listening SATs at KS3.
Art work	Permanent records of pupils' making and responding in the form of masks, collages, soundtracks, set or costume design, poetry or narrative.
Seminar/demonstration	Pupils research, plan and then lead group discussion on some aspect of drama, e.g. their research into a character, issue or historical period. Pupils physically demonstrate and comment on an aspect of their drama-making, the different ways a role could be played, or how they made a mask.
Self-evaluation profile	Pupils are regularly given a checklist of objectives for their work and offer a self-assessment of their progress and cite their own evidence to support their assessment. These self-assessments are agreed/not agreed by the teacher in discussion.

Drama and language development

So far, we have concentrated on the planned drama curriculum – a curriculum that is restricted to the formal study of selected concepts, practices, skills and experiences from the potential field of drama. In this section we are going to consider the interrelationship between drama and selected aspects of language and literacy development. We have noted that the positive benefits of using drama methods as part of the study of English and language arts is often an important consideration for schools. In many schools, drama is taught under the umbrella of English, by teachers whose first specialism is English. For these reasons, the planned drama curriculum may include additional aims and objectives which are related to an explicit focus on literacy and language development as part of drama.

Dramatic literature

There is a long tradition in English-speaking countries of studying and experiencing drama as part of the study of English language and literature. Historically, this is a reflection of the 'literary-ness' of the English speaking theatre. In a theatrical tradition that gives greatest value to the work of playwrights, it is inevitable that the study of dramatic literature should become part of English studies. It continues to be important to introduce pupils to historical and contemporary dramatic literature, both as drama and as literature. Such study gives pupils both the pleasure and challenge of a writer's work and also provides access to the performance codes and histories of the literary theatre. Understanding a writer's intention through close reading and then deconstructing it and physically reconstructing it as a performed text is an important learning process for pupils to follow.

Registers and codes of communication

Reading and performing extracts from dramatic literature represents an obvious relationship between English and drama, but in recent years this relationship has been extended in new directions. Increasingly, we have become aware of language as a socially constructed system. Our use of language is highly 'situational' and culturally determined. In other words, much of what we say and do is bound to the situations that we find ourselves in; different situations require different uses of language. It is through language that we make our private meanings public – communicable to others – and this making public depends on there being a shared set of linguistic resources among the communicating group. If I want to tell you what I'm thinking and feeling, I have to put it into a form of communication that we both understand and which is appropriate to the situation that we find ourselves in. If I have had a nasty car crash which has caused me distress, I might need to share this distress through communicating it to others. The form through which this communication takes place (and therefore the 'meaning' of distress that I communicate) will be different according to whether I am communicating with:

- the police at the scene of the accident
- staff at the hospital where I have been taken

- my family when I get home
- friends who phone to see if I'm all right
- my insurance agent who comes to inspect the damage
- the magistrates at a court hearing.

In addition to these possible 'speech events' there will also be the need to communicate through writing, and again each of the different events will require a different form of writing: the statement to the police, the report for the insurance cover, a letter to a friend. In a social theory of language – a theory that connects the way that we communicate with the social circumstances in which we communicate – the form of communication is referred to as *register*. There are three elements to register which when taken together provide a means of analysing communication events:

1. **Discourse:** What is the content that is being discussed? At first sight it might seem that in each of the examples I gave for the car crash, the discourse was the same. It was about my car crash. But, in fact, there may well be subtle differences of discourse. In talking to the police and the magistrates my discourse, or 'sub-text' in dramatic terminology, may actually be more to do with what an innocent victim I am rather than the details of the accident. In talking to my family, my discourse may be more to do with my need for a hug!

2. **Tenor**: What is the relationship that I am establishing with others? The examples range from establishing a formal, perhaps even deferential, relationship – with the police and magistrates for instance – through to the intimate relationship I wish to establish with family members.

3. **Mode:** What form, or genre, of communication is being used? We can make a basic distinction between talking and writing, but distinctions can also be made within these categories. Mode is the most culturally codified element of register. We have evolved certain conventions of communication which are 'appropriate' for certain kinds of events and not others. To be literate one must know of these coded forms, how to observe the conventions and when to use a particular form. As a literate member of my culture I understand that each of the examples that I have given will require different codified forms of communication:

- making a *statement* to the police
- giving *witness* in a court
- giving an *account* to the insurance company
- retelling the event as an *anecdote* for friends and family.

To be literate, in the sense that one can recognise, use and control register is to be socially powerful. It gives you control over the communication events that you encounter. This level of literacy and the power that it brings have traditionally been associated with the education and upbringing of particular social groups rather than others. In other words, some children are more likely to experience through family and schooling the nuances and variety of language registers in a culture than others. If you are brought up in a professional home where the family members possess a high level of literacy, you are more likely to have experienced a variety of registers of language use than if you are brought up in a family that has not traditionally been educated or experienced in using language in *different* situations for different purposes.

Because, as we have seen, drama is so 'situational' it provides a means of giving all pupils experience and knowledge of register. The examples of communication events related to the car crash can all be enacted and analysed in the classroom. The different modes of writing can all be incorporated into that drama. Through the construction and experience of different kinds of situation related to the same events, all pupils can experience the power of literacy.

In our lived experience we operate in various social roles, we choose and use different registers and adopt/switch dialects according to the experience of the situation we are in. This is also what happens in drama.

- *We imagine that we are in a different physical and social situation from that of the classroom.* In drama, language is only one of the forms used to represent the situation. We don't just talk ourselves into the context. We also make meaningful use of space, gesture and objects to define both the physical and the social elements of the situation.

- *We take on new roles.* What we say and do is determined by who we are in the drama and the demands of the situation that we face.

- *We interact with others.* We establish our social relationship with the other players through language and actions – the language we each use expresses our needs and intent in the drama but it also symbolises our position in the social structure and hierarchies of the drama. If my role is that of a lawyer, I choose my words to communicate information but I also choose them to show that I am lawyer – I will talk like a lawyer.

- *We learn new language from the experience.* The drama experience, like a life experience, becomes a personal resource which can help us grow in our knowledge and use of language.

Embodied language

We can talk about language in the abstract, but our lived experience of language is immediate and physical. One of the problems of cultural representation that drama solves is to provide a means of representation in the *present* tense: to show life as it is being lived rather than to report on events that have already been lived. Whatever form drama-making takes, the challenge is to 'embody' words and ideas. Taking a character from the page and turning it into a character on the stage means having to translate dialogue and stage directions into physical actions and reactions. The idea of Hamlet becomes a flesh-and-blood actual presence; we smell him and see his *physical* torment. In improvisation, when we are as uncertain of what others might say as we are in life, we are physically affected by what we say and what others say to us; we experience actual surprise, the sweat of tension, pain and sadness. In both forms of drama, we experience language but we also experience the 'experience' that language seeks to convey.

Deconstruction

In the processes of rehearsal, actors use the elements of drama – the conventions of time, space and presence – to deconstruct the texts they are working on, so that they can eventually be reconstructed as a performance text. The purpose of rehearsal and workshops is to explore meanings, characters and ideas and try out possible interpretations. Rather than discussing interpretation, actors use drama – use role and space and time – to reveal the nuances of text. In the same way, pupils can use the conventions of drama as a means of exploring and discovering what lies beneath the surface of the texts they engage with in the English classroom. They can:

- enact scenes in the original text;
- take on roles from the text and be questioned about motives and intentions;
- use space and objects (including costume) in a variety of realist and symbolist ways to represent meanings in the text; to physically represent the psychic or cultural distance between characters, for instance;
- create 'missing' scenes or moments that are suggested but not fleshed out in the original text;
- explore how to use gesture to convey 'sub-text'; how inner speech can be visibly played, for instance;
- script, or improvise, alternative scenes or endings;
- demonstrate to each other that there can be a variety of 'possibles' when it comes to the interpretation and representation of meanings (different groups will respond to the same task in different ways).

Drama provides pupils with an immediate and physical means of getting to grips with texts and textual representation. Most of what our pupils know of the world, they know through representations of it. Drama provides pupils with a way of reconstructing the experience that is represented. This process causes them to become more conscious of 'voice' – the ideological interests of the text's producer.

Drama and writing

Just as working in drama can help pupils to turn abstract ideas and written language into concrete and living representations, so it can also help them to translate lived experience into a variety of written representations. There are pragmatic and pedagogical reasons for encouraging this process. Drama, in its live forms, is the most ephemeral of arts. It exists only in the moment of performance. Written outcomes provide a permanent and visible record of a pupil's progress and learning in drama. Writing may also help pupils to reflect and deepen their response to drama they have made or watched. The drama itself may provide a logic and purpose for writing in genres that pupils might otherwise find tedious – reports, arguments, letters. In the table below, I have drawn on KS3 pupils' own reflections about how drama helps them with writing. The pupils were grouped in three ability bands based on an assessment of writing samples. While the charts focus on writing, they also serve as a good general summary of how drama can help pupils in English.

Those pupils who are most challenged by writing responded particularly well to:	
the non-threatening, 'can do', climate of the drama	Drama is a spoken art. Young people are at home with using interpersonal language in social situations – it is their most familiar experience of language. The pupil's exchange of meanings in drama is not as exposed to failures of technical accuracy as it is in reading and writing activities
collaborating on ideas and acting out in groups	Drama is a social art form. It is realised through collaboration. Young people support the development of each other's skills by pooling their resources and ideas in the drama – individuals have this social resource to draw on for their own written response
being able to use objects and furniture to represent places and ideas before describing them in writing	Selecting and using visual and concrete symbols is easier than using the abstract systems of symbolic language. Choosing the right piece of furniture for a character, deciding on a photograph that might symbolise an event or a memory gives young writers material to translate into writing
the story form of drama which held their interest	Narratives are a very familiar and accessible means of ordering and presenting experience. In drama the story is physically acted out and the tensions and emotions of the story are emphasised. The story of the drama, together with its appeal, can be used to provide a context for a specific piece of writing, e.g. trial notes, coroner's report, economic prediction
the chance to 'hot-seat' characters, i.e. to interview someone in role	Finding out about a character by asking questions and listening to and watching the responses the character makes helps pupils to differentiate and complicate their character descriptions. Seeing a character will flesh out, literally, the pupils' own ideas
In the middle of the range, pupils responded particularly well to:	
the social realism of the theme and the form of the drama	Drama allows pupils to explore personal and social issues which are meaningful for them in the context of relationships – bullying, family politics, racism, personal identity. Pupils enjoy the realism of drama but also enjoy the tensions and heightened emotions. In drama, pupils explore the role of feelings in our thinking and doing

becoming emotionally engaged with the theme through the drama	Drama personalises abstract themes and concepts. A drama about racism will involve pupils in acting out or responding to the lives of those who are affected by it – they will feel for the characters in the drama as a means of coming to think more about the theme of the drama. Even if pupils go on to write an impersonal piece of writing – a school anti-racist policy for example – they will be charged with the emotions of the drama
discovering more about a character or situation through taking part in improvisations	Drama is always dialogic – made from many voices. Each role will see events differently and will respond differently. This helps pupils to see an event from a range of different points of view. Pupils discover more about their character from the way other role players respond to them. This experience helps pupils who are looking to include a wider range of perspectives and more fully rounded characters in their writing
negotiating first drafts for writing based on the experience of the drama	Drama represents social experiences, structures and processes. Pupils become involved in human situations which offer a wide variety of writing opportunities. A drama situation may produce letters, journals, legal documents, scripts, narrative. Pupils can negotiate their own writing from a wide range of alternatives and compare their chosen genre and register with peers who may have chosen a different form of writing based on the same drama situation
personal response/journal writing which allows for subjective responses to the drama work	Pupils enjoyed the social and collaborative nature of meaning-making in drama but also needed to interpret the drama for themselves, in their own individual voice. Personal response writing allows pupils to reflect on their feelings about the drama and to build personal interpretations of what might happen next
At the top end of the ability range, pupils responded particularly well to:	
looking for sub-text in the gestures and action of improvisation	Pupils enjoyed building ironies and contradictions into their role play by using the non-verbal signs of gesture and space to counterpoint the language or to give it nuance. This helped pupils to think about referencing non-verbal signs in their writing – to describe the discomfort an apparently confident character is experiencing, for instance
recognising and introducing symbols and metaphors into the drama; being aware of the drama as an artistic text open to crafting and interpretation	Although drama is realised through interpersonal speech and life-like actions, it is a textual form. Pupils enjoyed elaborating the drama as a text with layers of meaning, motifs, key symbols and themes. For these pupils, involvement in the drama was very close to 'reading' and 'writing' in the literary sense. This experience helped pupils to think of structure and metaphor in their own writing

finding and using appropriate registers for writing based on the teacher's model of language used in the improvisation	Pupils enjoyed the challenge of writing in unfamiliar registers and genres of writing when these registers and genres were suggested by the logic of the drama and used by the teacher in role, e.g. writing in the voice of a boss, legal dispositions needed for a courtroom scene, imitating historical language and documents
being interviewed by others in role as a way of stretching their own understanding of the character they were playing	Articulate pupils enjoyed the challenge of being 'hot-seated' in role and needing to keep in role whatever they might be asked by the others. Having to respond to questioning intuitively and credibly helped to confirm the pupils' sense of a character and gave them material for character development in their writing
scripting scenes to be used in the drama, or having their writing used to further develop the drama	Writing produced in response to the drama can be reintroduced into the drama as a means of moving the action on. A letter written by a pupil might be read in role by one of the characters. A diary entry might be read out as a starting point for the next improvisation. Any form of document or written text can be used as part of the story of the drama

The living experience of drama

So far we have concentrated on the subject of drama: on the codes of production and reception, the histories and skills of drama, which exist independently of learners and which need to be acquired. The drama curriculum needs to be explicit in terms of what aspects of the subject will be taught, but it also needs to be explicit about the role that drama will play in the lives of pupils. The pupils are the subjects of drama in schools. Through making, performing and responding to drama, they are given the chance to discover more about themselves, other people and the world that they share. There is, then, the lived experience of the drama curriculum, which will be different for different pupils. Through their physical participation in drama activities and through their physical experience of drama events in the school, pupils learn not just what drama is, but also what it does: the role that drama serves in our cultures.

In this sense, drama in schools is like the drama of traditional societies; it both reflects and makes community. In the past and in the present, communities have seen drama as performing important cultural and civic ends. Drama has been, and can still be, an important means of making the hidden influences of a community's culture visible, discussible and changeable. Drama represents how we live, how we have come to live this way, and how we might live differently. It both uses and comments on the webs of rules, conventions, status, traditions, collective identities, taboos and other shared meanings that constitute a community's culture. Making drama involves pupils in discussing and commenting on these cultural concepts. It allows them to 'play' with images of who they are and who they are becoming, to invent alternatives and to physically experience the difference of being 'someone else'. The production and performance of drama is also a form of community making. It requires a community (which might be a class or a school play production group) to work together towards a shared experience in which the communal goal is placed before individual interests.

The influence that drama might have on the culture of a school and its pupils is difficult to express in terms of concrete aims and objectives, but for many schools this is the most important contribution that drama makes. It is similar, in this respect, to sports. Both are social and physical activities. Both are valued for the contribution that they make to the pupils' physical, personal and social development rather than for vocational or academic reasons. Both involve the community and project the school's image through plays and matches. In many schools it is the *doing* of sports and the arts and the personal benefits that come from being involved that are valued above their importance as formal subjects.

As we noted earlier, a school's drama curriculum can and should combine local and national priorities. The curriculum model for drama in this book is a synthesis of guidance offered at a national level, but the lived curriculum needs to be locally defined and experienced. In general terms, however, there are three broad areas of cultural learning that pupils might experience in drama, or that teachers might aim to provide through their delivery of the drama curriculum. These three areas are: boundaries; public and private lives; and citizenship.

Boundaries

Whatever form drama takes it challenges us to explore, recognise and extend our physical, emotional and cognitive boundaries: the boundaries between what is me and what is not; what I feel confident to do and not confident to do; what I know about myself and others and what I don't.

The first boundary that pupils encounter is between watching and doing. Many pupils may come to drama with a strong sense of boundary between these two activities. To get up and physically participate in drama in front of one's peers is an important social boundary to cross. Pupils may also need to explore and recognise their own physical boundaries – what they are prepared to do and not do. Some pupils may be comfortable with realistic role-play but feel exposed, inhibited and vulnerable in dance or more abstract acting styles. Practical work in drama challenges the pupils to extend their physicality into more expressive and public behaviour.

Drama provides the space for pupils to explore their own identities – the boundary between what is me, what is other – through working on the problems of creating and representing roles and characters. Creating a character is a process of creating a fictional identity which is both different from and the same as oneself. When an actor plays Ophelia, the character that we see physically on stage is not the actor herself, but it is also not-not the actor herself. We enter into role, we project an external image of another person but in doing so we bring something of ourselves to the character; this is why different actors can play the same character in different ways. In making and taking roles, pupils discover that they will sometimes identify closely with the role they are creating and at other times they will strongly disassociate themselves from the role's attitudes and behaviours. These are concrete **acts of identity**. In drama, pupils have the chance to explore their emergent identities through reflecting on the acts of identification and non-identification that they make during the drama.

Feeling comfortable with experiencing and expressing emotions in public is also an important boundary to cross for many pupils. Schools are not generally conducive to such behaviour. Pupils themselves may be fearful of public expressions of feeling lest they should appear weak and vulnerable to their peers. The curriculum tends not to prioritise the engagement and expression of feelings in the classroom. The ability to feel, and to express feelings to others, is an important social and aesthetic quality.

Private and public lives

We all live in two worlds: the public and the private. The public refers to our social lives and public behaviour and the private to the intimacies of our family lives and our own solitude and inner speech. This distinction is of great importance in drama for two reasons.

In different ways, drama has shown us how people behave in response to the circumstances they find themselves in. This helps us to understand the extent to which our social lives are culturally constructed. In most public situations we have a set of cultural agreements about how we should behave and treat others. These agreements provide a framework of rules that are impersonal, i.e. expected of everyone. The language and behaviour of the courtroom is different from that of the dance floor. The more that pupils understand that so much of their adult lives will be spent in situations that require appropriate language and actions, the more prepared they will be to adopt (or challenge) the roles and responsibilities of public life. Drama can also provide pupils with an alternative experience of situations. If they take on the role of someone who is different from themselves in terms of status, gender, age or culture, they will also experience and use different language and behaviour.

Secondly, drama does not just represent the relationship between behaviour and social circumstances, it also comments on and interprets this relationship. The focus might be on revealing the oppressive circumstances that cause a young woman to accept an arranged marriage even though, privately, she doesn't want to. The focus might be on a specific aspect of situational behaviour such as status, environment, cultural difference. In order to explore the relationship between social behaviour and circumstances, drama often concentrates on the troubled margins between the public and the private, the difficulties caused by the interpenetration of the two worlds. One only has to think of the conflicts between private desires and public duties experienced by Macbeth, Hamlet and Lear. The most interesting place for pupils to explore the private and the public is where they collide. There have been frequent occasions when my life as a teacher has collided with my private life, and each occasion has generated enough material for several dramas.

Pupils are intensely aware of the distinction between the private and the public in their lives. Schools are public places which pupils need to negotiate. They understand the dangers of disclosing the private to the public scrutiny of their peers and their teachers. Sometimes these dangers seem so great to pupils that they will avoid any public behaviour in case it is read as a sign of the private, or leads to discussion of the private – the fear of answering questions or volunteering to help, lest you are accused of being a 'nerd' or 'teacher's pet'. In the classroom, teachers can contract and police a public world that protects the pupils' privacy while providing the rules, codes, manners to facilitate the involvement of pupils without threat. Elsewhere in the school, they may feel more vulnerable and less protected by formal agreements about behaviour. Drama can draw pupils' attention to the need to establish, among themselves, a set of rules for public behaviour in school that respects the privacy and rights of others: a highway code that allows all to safely negotiate the playground.

Citizenship

There is an important relationship between the active participation in the public forum of drama and the active involvement of citizens in maintaining and extending democracy. Like participatory drama, democracies require the active involvement of citizens who are willing to put the common good before their own interests and to take whatever actions are needed to ensure the protection of the democratic virtues of equality, justice and freedom. Like drama, democracy is practised socially and in *public* – in debates, meetings, demonstrations, committees.

The roles that pupils take in drama at KS3 are often citizen roles. They are faced with problems, dilemmas or conflicts of interest in the drama that require them to act collectively rather than in their own private interest. The difference between what is best for me and what is best for the community is a dilemma commonly explored in drama. A drama may also challenge pupils to face the problems of difference. How do we decide what's best when we have so many different ideas and different people to consider? How would I feel about what is happening in the drama if I was of a different gender, age, ability, culture?

In some cases, drama will directly serve democratic processes in the school. Drama might be used, for instance, as part of an anti-bullying strategy to provide a public forum for pupils to represent, debate and try out strategies for ridding the school of anti-democratic behaviours. The sacrifices of time and the personal responsibility to the collective that pupils take in order to be involved in a school play are also like the sacrifices that individuals must make in order to serve as citizens.

2

The roles, skills and knowledge of the drama teacher

In this section I am going to look at the roles, skills and knowledge of a drama teacher. My interest is in identifying what a potential drama specialist might need in addition to the skills and knowledge required of any competent and qualified teacher. All teachers, for instance, must have knowledge of the subject they are going to teach and know how to apply this knowledge in the classroom. They must be experienced in basic classroom management and planning schemes of work that are relevant and appropriate to the pupils they teach. They must know how to assess, report and record the achievements of their pupils.

This section assumes, then, that the potential drama specialist is starting from a base of good practice. The additional roles, skills and knowledge that a drama teacher must develop are not necessarily unique to drama. Teachers in other Arts subjects will also be developing similar competencies, as will sports teachers who share a similar dual role as classroom teacher and extra-curricular tutor.

Roles

Manager

The drama teacher needs to be able to manage time, space and bodies and to do so in both the social dimension of the classroom and in the aesthetic dimension of the art-form. We have already noted that time, space and presence are the key elements of drama and that the study and experience of drama is tied to understanding, controlling and using these elements, in all their variety, to create drama.

But the elements of drama are also the problematic elements of the social encounter with pupils in drama lessons. In most other subjects, pupils enter into classrooms where space is controlled by the layout of desks and other furniture. Their movement around the classroom is restricted by the simple instruction to remain seated. Their behaviour can also be controlled by the use of text books and individual, silent study. 'Sit down, no talking, open your books at page 33 and complete the exercises. There is no need for anyone to get up; you're working on your own so I don't want to hear any talking.' The usual control mechanisms of the classroom allow teachers to work with individuals, to control groups and to quickly establish their authority. It is also the case that, in most subjects, even the most reluctant pupils can be pressured into completing work – either in class, at home or in some form of detention.

In contrast, the drama teacher usually works in large open spaces with large numbers of pupils in short periods of time. The space, the pupils and the teacher are the material for the lesson – it is rare to find drama being taught from textbooks in the conventional manner – it is a practical subject. Nor can pupils be forced to do drama – take roles and make enactments – against their consent. These characteristics of the drama lesson make additional demands on a teacher's existing classroom management skills. The mode of management that will be used is the **contract** and we will return to the skills of contracting later.

There are certain management principles that can assist teachers in making effective use of the time and space and physical behaviours of pupils in drama lessons.

Element	Principles
space	Make sure that the space for drama is clean, well prepared and cleared of everything but the essential furniture or equipment required for the lesson. Pupils will pick up on the signs the space gives them. If it is messy, dirty and neglected, pupils will respond accordingly!
	Anticipate the problems the space might create. Begin lessons with a formal use of the space; have the pupils enter and sit in a formal circle of chairs (or on the floor) or have groups of chairs prearranged if the lesson begins with group work.
	Establish clear boundaries for pupil work; place groups yourself so that they are not too crowded or too distant; make corners, levels and dangerous space off-limits; insist on pupils working within the space that has been allocated so that they don't interfere with other groups.
time/tasks	Give groups clear objectives and an expectation of the outcome of group work. Set and keep to time limits for each group task.
	Anticipate potential problems of noise, aggressive behaviour and uncontrolled use of space and furniture by including constraints in the briefing for group work: I want you to ... I don't want you to ... This isn't an opportunity to have a fight and roll all over the floor ... I don't want to see anyone crossing over into another group's space ...
	Consider carefully how a scheme of work will be broken up into lesson-units. Where do the natural breaks occur? How can the endings, beginnings and homework be used to strengthen links between lessons which may be a week apart? Begin lessons by having pupils recap from last lesson, end by anticipating how the work will develop in the next lesson. Give pupils questions to consider or homework related to the drama (e.g. writing in role, making a map or mask) between lessons.
	Vary the experience of time so that there is an enjoyable and satisfying balance between the quiet, reflective and slow analysis of the relationship between time, space and presence, and busy, energetic episodes when the drama may move forward more rapidly.

behaviour Carefully consider the size and composition of groups in terms of gender, ability, friendship groups, power dynamics.

Develop an explicit contract that is a negotiated and agreed set of rules or 'manners' to control, protect and respect the pupils.

Use a variety of groupings within the lesson; whole class, small elective groups, small selected groups, pairs.

Make sure that you know everyone's name! It is difficult to control individual behaviour without being able to name the individual. Identify leaders or key players in the group and work with them to gain respect and interest.

Isolate disruptive or negative pupils either by careful consideration of groupings – dispersed or contained in one group. Don't allow one or two pupils to prevent the rest from working. Avoid confrontation in front of the whole class by organising group work while you deal with disruptive pupils privately; keep them out of the group work until they have accepted your terms.

Don't try to force pupils to do drama. In group work allow pupils the possibility of contributing to the making without having to perform themselves. Pupils are more likely to perform if they don't have to!

Animateur

In many schools, drama is at best an optional activity that has a fairly marginal status within the curriculum. The role of the drama teacher will include being an animateur who seeks to develop drama in ways that begin to move drama from the margins to the core of the life of the school.

The drama teacher needs to be able to clearly advocate the unique contribution that drama makes to the curriculum. This will involve an assessment of the school's local priorities and how drama can make a direct contribution to them. We have already seen in the first chapter that schools place different values on drama – as a form of PSE or as an integral part of English, for instance. The drama teacher is likely to have to enter into long and difficult negotiations to gain extra curriculum time, or manageable time-periods and appropriate spaces. These priorities are unlikely to be in place unless a drama teacher has worked to establish them! Negotiating a place and time for drama is made easier by forming partnerships with other 'sympathetic' subject areas: English, Art and Music, for instance.

The drama teacher is also responsible for animating opportunities for extra-curricular drama activities through the creation of lunch-time or after-school clubs. These are entirely voluntary and enjoyable opportunities for pupils to pursue their vocational interest in doing drama. Setting up, running and maintaining extra-curricular drama makes considerable demands on a drama teacher's time and energy, but there are clear rewards also. A different kind of relationship and loyalty is established in extra-curricular work which will transfer back into curriculum drama – you will have 'friends' in the classroom. Extra-curricular work also gives drama a very visible and public face in the school – drama is seen to be doing a good job and the pupils' commitment and sacrifices will be noticed. You are reclaiming the traditional role of drama as a living community practice that both reflects and makes community.

The community dimension of drama in schools and, therefore, of the drama teacher's role will extend into work that is done with, and for, other groups in the community that the school serves. Productions are a popular way of bringing parents and families into the life of drama. School productions have an irreducible community element. They are local productions made by pupils who are also known to the audience as sons, daughters, neighbours, sisters. The response to school productions is often celebratory and filled with positive community pride rather than objectively critical. Pupils are given the opportunity to project a positive image of themselves, the school and the community they belong to. The best production work also draws on the hidden talents and strengths of other teachers who are not associated with drama but who have skills in design, lighting, costume or stage management. Production work may also be targeted at specific groups within the local community – the local primary and special schools, pensioners' clubs and cultural centres such as museums or galleries.

The drama teacher is also responsible for providing pupils with living examples of drama through organising visits to the theatre and for bringing touring theatre and performance work into the school. Carefully chosen theatre visits provide the means of bringing all pupils into the culture of theatre-going. The theatre can only be accessible to all if all are given access to it through education in its conventions and practice in theatre-going. Theatre work that is bought in, or visited, should reflect the cultural diversity of aesthetic traditions in this country. Pupils should experience African and Asian performance in addition to the mainstream and avant-garde Euro-American tradition of theatre.

Facilitator

According to the Oxford Dictionary, to facilitate is 'to make easy or less difficult or more easily achieved'. All teachers play the facilitator role: wanting to make it easier or less difficult for pupils to achieve their potential in a positive climate. Because drama is a social art that requires the physical involvement of its producers and because a class is already a social group that the pupils are physically involved in, the drama teacher needs to be able to facilitate the working dynamics of both kinds of group – the group that comes through the door and the group working together on the production of drama. There has to be a recognition and facilitation of the central paradox of drama teaching. The first condition of theatre is that it is *by choice*. In schools, particularly at KS3, pupils are often required to do drama. They have no choice.

There are three aspects to the facilitation of this paradox:

1. a clear and visible priority is given to the pupils' lived experience of the drama curriculum and there is a willingness to diverge from or modify the planned curriculum as a result of this experience;

2. the creation and maintenance of a regulated 'public world' in the drama classroom;

3. a high degree of tolerance and skill in managing and allowing pupil choices about the form and content of the work.

A practical drama lesson has to be planned in a way that allows pupils to become comfortably and confidently involved as the lesson progresses. The sequencing and staging of the learning process of the lesson – the realising of the objectives – has to be mediated through the imperative of making the pupils' lived experience of drama comfortable enough for them to want to join in. Whatever the planned objectives might be, the pupils' inhibitions, physical embarrassment, fear of censure, transient moods and relationships to others in the group need to be taken into account.

The drama teacher needs to be able to make an accurate reading of the class as a social group, the individuals in the group and their relationships to the group as a whole. This is not a psychological reading, a guess at what is going on inside each pupil. It is an assessment of a group's culture and the social roles that pupils play within this culture. The drama teacher's concern is with the relationship *between* pupils: their public and social interpersonal behaviours. In their experience of the public world of school, individual pupils express their personal needs through the roles they choose, or are given, within the culture of the groups they belong to.

These individual needs might include the need:

- to belong
- to contribute
- for recognition
- for anonymity
- for status
- for power
- for dependency
- for freedom
- for recognition of particular problems.

The expression of these needs through 'role-behaviour' (behaviour that is specific to the group and to the classroom situation) may have both positive and negative manifestations. In the table that follows I have tried to categorise the social roles that pupils might adopt, and to describe the positive and negative behaviours associated with the roles taken.

Positive behaviours	Social roles	Negative behaviours
Respond well to the responsibility of managing group work and getting the job done. Have the respect of others in the group. Once they are 'on-side' with ideas and objectives, others will follow	**leaders**	Use their status within the group to challenge the teacher's authority. Others in the group are forced to choose between following peer-leader or following teacher. Gate-keepers who will prevent others joining in. Physically and vocally dominate discussion and practical work

Willing to adapt to and compromise with others. Do not pursue their own need for power. Will accept direction from others and are satisfied with helping to realise another pupil's ideas	**followers**	Rarely initiate ideas or contribute to discussion and planning. Wait for others to get involved and take risks. Become 'stooges' for negative leaders. Develop a habit of non-participation. Fail to 'taste' leadership
Debunk pretentiousness; bring a raw, earthy and healthy disrespect to the work. Introduce ironies and parodic behaviour to lighten and relieve emotional pressure. Make the social experience of drama more enjoyable for all	**jokers**	Prevent or subvert serious, honest responses. Hide behind their humour. Ignore the sensitivities of other pupils. Distract groups from task. Distract the teacher with facile or petty physical and vocal responses
Can be trusted and relied on to fetch, carry, report, stay late to help out, send messages. The 'stage managers' of the group	**helpers**	Would rather help than do! Find other jobs to do while groups work on production of drama – cleaning out cupboards, stacking books. Seen as 'creeps'; compromise their own status within group
Get groups 'doing'. Help to move pupils out of their chairs into physical action. Keep the pace and rhythm of the class brisk and busy. Enjoy taking part and getting on with it	**doers**	Want to short circuit necessary discussion and planning. Commit too quickly to first idea offered. Impatient to show work before it is ready. Reluctant to watch and evaluate other groups' work
Have no positive role to play!	**negative spectators**	Remain on the outside of the work. Do not make any positive or active contribution but through body-language and insidious comments and asides seek to subvert the work of the teacher and the other pupils. Energy is expended on trying to make sure that nothing happens. May tease or threaten other pupils out of class for their willingness to be involved in drama

Sensitive and protective of the needs of individual group members. Monitor for signs of emotional distress or conflicts between the drama and other pupils' personal agendas. Sense and stand up for what is fair and just	**'sisters' and 'brothers'**	Over-protective and over-sensitive to the needs of others. May gossip or exaggerate personal problems. Raise personal or pastoral problems at inappropriate moments. Attribute personal motives for other pupils' choices of role and role behaviour in the drama
Make the teacher more conscious of group dynamics, individual needs. Resist cosy consensus and insist on individual difference and perspective	**loners**	Fear the social demands of drama. Suffer anxiety and fear exposure. Become more inhibited and more fearful of the public world because of their private experiences in drama class

Different teachers will have different ways of categorising and recognising the diversity of social roles in the class. And pupils don't come ready packaged into these roles!

There will also be local cultural and gender differences in the way that roles are played. But some awareness of the different functions that individuals play in the creation and maintenance of a group culture helps a teacher to

- manage the social dynamics
- allocate responsibilities
- support and challenge appropriately, and
- facilitate the social production of drama.

Drama both reflects and *makes* community. In its social production of drama the group will reflect its actual strengths and weaknesses, its patterns of power and domination, its habitual responses, its social health. But the way in which the teacher facilitates the social production of drama will make a difference to the class as a social group; there will be positive effects which are transferable to other social situations faced by the group.

In trying to accentuate the positive and eliminate the negative in social role behaviours the teacher may use a wide range of facilitator functions. The practical nature of most KS3 drama work means that some of these functions are related to ensuring the production of high-quality work during the lesson. The social nature of production in drama means that some functions are related to maintaining the social health and working effectiveness of the group. Below, I have summarised what some of these task and maintenance functions might be.

Facilitator functions

Task-related

initiating	proposing tasks or goals or actions, defining group problems, suggesting procedures
informing	supplying relevant facts and instructions, giving expression to feelings or opinions
seeking	asking for information, opinions, feelings, ideas from others to help group discussion and practice
clarifying	interpreting ideas or suggestions, defining terms and tasks, checking out group or individual issues
summarising	putting together related ideas, restating suggestions, offering a decision or conclusion for group to consider
testing for reality	asking the group to test what it is doing or saying by referring to known facts or source text in order to see if the group is behaving realistically/authentically
expediting	prodding the group to action or decision, encouraging groups to strive for quality in their work

Maintenance-related

harmonising	attempting to reconcile disagreements, reducing tension, getting pupils to explore and respect differences
gate-keeping	helping to keep communication channels open, facilitating participation, suggesting procedures that permit open sharing of agendas
consensus testing	testing a group's willingness to agree and the basis of such agreement – is it owned by the group or dominant individuals?
encouraging	being firm but friendly, warm and responsive to positive behaviour, indicating by facial expression or remark the acceptance of pupils' positive contributions
compromising	offering a compromise when own idea or status is in conflict with group's, modifying planned lesson in the interests of group cohesion or growth
process observing	watching how groups operate and sharing these perceptions with the groups
standard setting	expressing standard for the group to work by, testing behaviour against such standards
trust builder	accepting and supporting openness in group members, recognising and reinforcing risk-taking
interpersonal problem solver	promoting open discussion of conflicts between group members in order to resolve conflicts and increase group cohesiveness, involving group in maintenance and enforcement of contract

Actor/dramaturge

Making and performing drama is at the heart of the drama curriculum. In some cases the drama will be based on the realisation of an existing playtext (script/dramatic literature); in others the drama will be devised from the exploratory work of pupils and may be based on a non-dramatic source such as a story, poem, image or abstract theme. In both forms of drama there are two kinds of text in play: the **source text** and the **performance text**.

The performance text – what is actually said and done in performance – only exists in the time of performance whereas the source text remains. In our everyday experience of theatre we are conscious of the autonomy of the performance text every time we go to see a different production of a familiar work of dramatic literature. Our interest is in what a particular director and group of actors will *do* with a familiar text that might be different or that might offer a fresh interpretation.

In the modern Western theatre tradition two tendencies have developed in the making of performance texts. In the first, the producers (directors, actors, designers, etc.) are concerned to offer an authentic interpretation of the playwright's intentions – the performance text is a direct representation of the playwright's instructions to the producers (script, stage notes and directions contained in the original written score). In this literary form of theatre the audience judges the extent to which the performance text is 'faithful' to the original written score.

In the second tendency of performance text-making, the source text is only important in so far as it provokes or begins the devising of a performance which is as much a representation of the producers' own ideas and agendas as it is of ideas and agendas suggested by the author of the source text. The source text (where it exists) may be adapted, abridged, even subverted. The performance text may be built out of fragments of text from a variety of sources. If the literary tendency highlights the playwright as 'author', then this alternative tendency highlights the producers as 'auteurs'.

The term **dramaturgy** is used to describe the weaving together of stage actions into a unified performance text: its roots are in the Greek *drama-ergon* – the 'work of the actions'. A performance is made out of 'actions': not only what is said and done but also the sounds, lights, and changes in space. Even objects become actions in performance in the sense that they change the space they are placed in. But of course the 'actions' are not all simultaneously present – they are temporally and spatially sequenced to make a performance that unfolds in time. Dramaturgy, therefore, refers to the sequencing of actions both at particular moments in the performance and in the larger scale relationship between moments, which 'taken together' comprise the whole experience of a complete performance; we experience each passing moment of a performance but we also experience the developing structure as it gathers towards a sense of a 'finished' performance (which is the total and progressive effect of all the actions that together constitute a dramatic statement or experience).

This is the art of drama as a genre of performance rather than as a branch of literature – the intentional weaving together of stage actions in order to make a living and lived *experience* for an audience. At KS3 the drama teacher, as dramaturge, has two responsibilities: to initiate and develop the 'weave' of the drama, and to draw pupils' attention to that 'weaving' so that they begin to share in the teacher's knowledge and to make their own decisions about the 'weave'.

The weave that the drama teacher makes with pupils is dependent on **knowledge** of a wide variety of dramaturgical devices or conventions, drawn from both theatre traditions and also from film and TV conventions. It is also dependent on the skills of **structuring**, which refers to the ways in which the various conventions may be assembled and juxtaposed in order to create an aesthetic and educational experience for pupils. The role of the drama teacher as dramaturge is to use this knowledge and the skills of structuring *responsibly*. The teacher is responsible for the following aspects.

Developing and enhancing the artistic potential of pupils' ideas and responses

While discussion, negotiation, planning and researching are all important activities that go on in drama as they do in other subjects, the teacher's prime responsibility is to facilitate the move into using the codes of theatre production as the main activity in drama. This means being able to translate the pupils' intentions and suggestions, or the subject objectives for the lesson, into dramatic ideas and processes. To see, for instance, how discussion about human experiences can become a dramatic realisation of imagined experience – roles, situations, gestures, symbols, contrasts – or to choose dramatic literature that is appropriate to the needs and interests of the pupils.

In mainstream theatre the actor is the prime signifier. Whatever else is used in terms of props, costume, lighting and spatial design it is principally the actor who draws our attention and who generates and communicates dramatic intentions and possibilities. Pupils at KS3 are unlikely to have the trained body of an actor or to be able to match the expressive powers of an actor. The teacher needs to make greater use of props, lighting, sound and other non-physical properties to reinforce and support pupils as actors. The teacher may also use her own skills of acting as a model of status and register:

- to demonstrate a character's response to the given circumstances of the dramatic context;
- to initiate role responses, or to offer cues for other actors to follow;
- to transform (through her own physical and psychic transformation into character) the actual world of the classroom into a fictional world or context.

The uses of 'teacher-in-role', as a dramaturgical device, is one of the most important contributions that drama education has made to the world of theatre.

Managing the constraints of time, space and numbers

As well as aspiring to art-making, the drama must also take account of the logistics of the lesson – the time available, the limitations of the space provided and the need to actively include as many pupils as possible in the drama.

This consideration, in part, accounts for the difference between dramaturgy in the classroom and in other genres of theatre. The relatively short duration of a drama class has meant that drama teachers have developed particular conventions that can be quickly produced without the need for lengthy preparations or rehearsal: tableau, improvisation, hot-seating, etc. Using these conventions a teacher can provide pupils with a variety of different activities in the space of a single lesson.

Space is one of the elements of drama but many lessons have to be taught in classrooms or small spaces which don't permit movement or a creative use of space. In these circumstances the dramaturgy has to focus on time and role and an imagined, or mentally constructed, 'picture' of space to make drama.

Few mainstream plays make use of thirty or more actors working as an ensemble! The drama teacher has to structure in a way that allows for every pupil to be involved. This may entail varying the size of groups, rotating or doubling-up key roles or organising group work so that different aspects or episodes of the narrative are worked on simultaneously. The advantage of having six or seven small groups is that they will produce a range of different responses to the drama – *different* tableaux, roles, situations, etc. This range of difference is a positive aspect in the dramaturgy.

Balancing the planned curriculum against the local needs and lived experience of pupils

Working with pupils in the classroom is very different from working with actors who are either professionally or vocationally motivated. A director can expect professional actors to deal with their emotional responses to the material that is being dramatised. S/he can also expect actors to attempt what is required and to accept critical feedback during rehearsal and performance and to maintain professional working relations with other actors. The same cannot be expected of pupils.

In drama education the pupils often need to be lured or persuaded to take part and the teacher needs to carefully consider the level of personal challenge that the work presents. The pupils' actual emotional responses to the material that is being dramatised often become the focus of the work. The subjective feelings that pupils experience become the basis for their emotional understanding of the material and the human experience it suggests. It is this subjective understanding, which in other styles of acting leads to an objective characterisation, that is of interest to the teacher.

Drama is a powerful medium for exploring and representing human experiences. The teacher needs to use it responsibly so that pupils feel stretched but not threatened by the emotional intensity of the work. The teacher needs to respect pupils' vulnerabilities and insecurities about using their bodies expressively in front of their peers and to understand that problematic relationships in the class are unlikely to be put on hold for drama.

Skills

Questioning

Drama is a questioning medium. It seeks to disturb, extend or change our understanding of who we are and who we are becoming. Drama tends to focus on those moments of experience which forcefully reveal the paradoxes and ambiguities of human actions and reactions; those moments which provoke us to ask questions about ourselves and the worlds in which we live.

In order to respond to these questions, pupils use a logic based on their prior cultural and narrative experiences. In other words, pupils' responses to the questions raised by a drama may draw on their knowledge of similar narratives and how they can be expected to turn out and they may also draw on their existing cultural understanding of how people are likely to act and react in the given circumstances of the drama. It is the teacher's responsibility to help pupils to operate these logical systems and to apply them to the drama as it unfolds. Through questioning, the teacher helps pupils to make sense and make connections. The teacher's questions also reveal differences and ambiguities in the pupil's responses. In the social art of drama, meanings are not privately held or formed; they are established collectively through debate and through the dialogue that is established by the teacher's questioning of the sense-making that the group does.

The questioning of the human condition that underpins drama flows through the modes of making, performing and responding.

In *making* drama, pupils work at discovering and exploring both the means and the meanings that will form the dramatic representation of a particular experience. The relationships between character, context and action, and dramatic conventions are forged through detailed research that corresponds to the rehearsal process in mainstream theatre. Theatre work which is based on extensive exploratory rehearsal is sometimes referred to as **laboratory theatre**: a theatre in which dramatic means are used to research, test and develop our understandings of human nature and culture. To create a character, the young actor must ask questions about what will make the character recognisably different from the actor's own character. How do I communicate this 'otherness'? How will this 'other' person respond in ways which are psychologically, culturally and historically true to the given circumstances of the drama? This making of character will also raise questions for the young actor about the parameters of their own identity – how would I respond in the same circumstances?

In *performing* drama, pupils seek to convey their understandings and findings through characterisation and actions which are selected as being concrete examples of their ideas about the experience that is being represented. These examples of character and behaviour provoke the 'W' questions (see below) that an audience seeks answers to as the drama unfolds. In the modern Western theatre tradition, we deduce the inner lives of characters from the external gestures and visible responses that the actor selects as being 'significant' of character. The patterns of gesture and response that the actor creates are often inconsistent or paradoxical or surprising, so that the audience is left with complex questions about why people behave as they do and how they are shaped by cultural circumstances. Actors may behave 'as if' they were someone else in another time and place, but only so as to raise for the audience the open-ended question – what if ...?

In *responding* to drama, pupils need to ask the questions that will help them to unravel the human puzzle that is presented on stage. When we see a play performed for us, we make sense of the drama that is being presented through piecing together the clues and cues that answer our questions:

What is happening?
Who is involved?
Where and When is it happening?
What has happened to create this moment?
What will happen next?

The drama teacher works alongside the pupils, using questions to discover the sense they are making of the dramatic experience. Without asking, the drama teacher cannot know what individuals think, how they respond, what connections they are making with their own experience or what ideas they might want to try out. There must be a genuine attempt by the teacher to see the dramatic experience from the pupils' perspective – to understand and work within their view of the world. This projection is not unlike the projection that producers must make in order to ensure that the meanings of the drama are communicated effectively to an audience.

The questions that are selected might fulfil a variety of functions in the drama lesson:

Clarifying: checking pupils' responses; confirming where pupils are with the drama; checking that instructions have been understood

Inferring asking how the gestures and actions the pupils are using are tied to the 'meanings' which they want to communicate; checking out the teacher's perceptions of the work with the pupils

Probing drawing pupils' attention to the consequences or implications of their actions/ideas; testing commitment or understanding; pushing pupils to deeper levels of engagement

Challenging checking prejudicial or culturally specific attitudes or ideas; questioning the social dynamics of the group; encouraging the group to go beyond the surface of experience

Reality-checking asking the group to test their ideas or work against their own sense of reality and logic.

Different questions elicit different responses from pupils. There are obvious distinctions to be made between open questions which do not predetermine a response and closed questions which contain assumptions about the response expected. The root word of a question will also determine the response that is made. Below I have categorised different root words in questions and the responses they are likely to get.

What ...?	*asks pupils to itemise or list* – what do you need? What is X scared of? What will his daughter say when she finds out?
When/Where/Which?	*asks pupils for specific information* – When is this happening? Where would she sit? Which of these two chairs would make the best throne?
How ...?	*asks pupils to reveal processes and feelings* – how are agreements made in this family? How would she feel about what he is doing? How can we represent that idea?
Could/Would ...?	*tests potential* – Would she still come back after all she has heard? Would you behave in the same way yourself? Could you imagine that it might be different?
Should ...?	*asks for moral judgement* – Should he have spoken to his mother in that way? Should anyone make that demand on another? Should we try and listen to each other?
Why ...?	*asks for explanations* – Why doesn't she answer the question? Why is the king so angry with his daughters? Why are you finding it so difficult to play the character?

Contracting

We have already noted that pupils can't be made to do drama in the same way that they can be made to write or to complete textbook exercises. There has to be an agreement to do drama. This agreement is easier to make if there is a visible and negotiable framework of ground rules, codes of conduct and behavioural objectives. The framework serves the same purpose as the rules of a game. The 'players' know that the rules of the 'game' provide a safe and fair means of becoming involved. Knowing what to expect from others and what is expected of you gives confidence, security and protection. Knowing what the rules are and what happens if you, or others, 'cheat' removes the fear of getting it wrong. In every classroom teachers will use an agreed sanctions system to protect the climate for learning. The contract in drama may include the sanctions system but it is more than that – it represents an ongoing dialogue about how to maintain the quality of learning and interpersonal relationships in drama.

'Dialogue' implies that pupils are also contributing to the contract. They have the opportunity to protect themselves and to establish a culture for the drama class that will make it safer for them to engage with the drama-making. The concerns that pupils might have will include, what will happen if:

- people laugh at me?
- no one wants to work with me?
- I reveal something that might be used against me?
- no one listens to my ideas?
- I feel uncomfortable about my body?
- I just don't feel like it today?
- people in the group ignore me, or disrupt my work?
- the drama touches a raw nerve?

- the drama disturbs my cultural beliefs?
- I don't agree with what we're doing?

These are all possibilities which the drama teacher needs to be aware of and to discuss with the group. This discussion might lead to decisions and social agreements about what will happen if any of these concerns emerge. The nature of the concerns that pupils might have results from the particular characteristics of making, performing and responding in drama.

Drama requires trust, trust involves taking risks

Contracting recognises the risks involved for both teacher and pupil and seeks to limit the risk by defining and proscribing behaviour which will break teacher–pupil and pupil–pupil trust.

Drama requires the public presentation of private states of being or feeling

Actors need to express a wide range of emotions, but the peer and institutional culture of schools seeks to suppress or censure expressions of strong emotions. Contracting legitimises and protects the expression of feelings and recognises that the emotions that pupils express as characters are not to be read as signs of the actor's own character. If the actor is required to cry, it doesn't make the actor a 'cry-baby'!

Drama draws attention to the actor's use of body to physicalise meanings and therefore attention is drawn to the actor's body

The actor's fictive use of the body is the central signifier in drama. Contracting rejects the idea that you must look like, be the same age/culture/gender as, the character you will physicalise – anyone can take any part. Contracting also disallows comments about other pupils' bodies and allows pupils to discuss their own tolerance levels in physically demanding work.

Drama is socially produced; individuals are asked to put the common 'good' or goals before their own private interests

Drama belongs to the public sphere of our lives. Just as in other public, or civic, practices we are asked to observe certain conventions and to put the communal needs and goals before our own private interests. Contracting stresses the need for us to work for the good of us all rather than to pursue personal agendas and priorities.

The drama seeks to make connections with the public self and the private me of the actor and the audience

We see ourselves in the drama; its representations may seem to touch on our most private and intimate lives or comment on the presentation of self as bully or victim or cheat. Contracting ensures that all activity in drama is masked – there is no need to declare or probe into the private world of the pupil.

The teacher's contracting in drama may serve different pedagogic purposes:

Framing	*Setting the parameters of pupil/teacher behaviours* – use of space, noise levels, productivity levels, clarifying objectives, courtesies, and sanctions system
Anticipating	*Pre-empting likely problems* – talking about specific control/space/personal and interpersonal problems likely to be encountered in the work
Trouble-shooting	*Applying the contract* – defusing and managing breaches of contract by referring back to the agreements that have been made and asking for them to be complied with (the contract becomes an impersonal regulator)
Taking collective responsibility	*Sharing the maintenance of the contract* – open discussion of problems and breaches of contract with the expectation that the class, as well as the teacher, are responsible for settling difficulties.

There are two important considerations for any teacher who wishes to establish contracting as a means of classroom management.

1. *Start as you mean to go on!* It's important to establish contracting with pupils as soon as they enter the new school at KS3. The behavioural problems of 11-year-olds may not seem as difficult to manage as those of 14–15-year-olds. Firmly establishing a contract at the outset will prevent problems emerging later in the pupil's career.

2. *Never give up!* It takes time to create a learning community in which individuals regulate their own behaviour and negotiate the climate for learning. Pulling a group into shape can be a long and difficult process – but you have to hold on to the vision that contracting offers! Why else be a teacher!

Structuring

Some of the work that a drama teacher does will be in the form of lessons that are planned in ways which would be familiar to teachers of other subjects – lessons on aspects of theatre history, stage craft or technology for instance. But, as we noted in the discussion of the teacher's role as dramaturge, there is an expectation that making and experiencing drama is at the heart of the drama curriculum.

The quality of the making and experiencing is, at first, dependent on the teacher's skills of structuring. During KS3, the teacher's modelling of structure and the choices that are available in structuring a dramatic experience will merge into the expectation that the pupils will become increasingly confident, knowledgeable and responsible for their own structuring.

In a conventional lesson plan, activities are organised so that pupils can understand, internalise and apply the particular skill, concept or knowledge that is contained in the lesson's objectives. On the surface, a planned drama experience may look like a conventional plan. The teacher will have aims and objectives for the session and will also have a list, or sequence, of activities for the pupils to engage with. But, in addition to satisfying the curriculum objectives for the lesson, the sequence must also provide pupils with a living experience of drama – an analogous experience to being in or at a play or watching an episode of drama in some other form. The sequencing of the lesson needs to be as subtle and as crafted as any other dramatic sequence which is planned to unfold its meanings, or theme, in time and space and which moves the audience, progressively, towards a new-felt understanding of the human issues and themes that are being dramatised.

In this sense the structure of the classroom drama is in the form of a **montage:** a construction of meanings which is a specific result of the assembly of form and content during a drama. The montage, or the juxtaposing of the 'pieces' used in the drama, also guides pupils through the dramatic event or experience. The montage is more than the linear sequence of events in the narrative. In theatre, the events of the story are only one dimension of the presentation. Theatre is a spatial as well as a temporal art. What happens in the theatre space, in terms of objects, design, lighting, sound and the physical arrangement and gestures of the players also contributes to our understanding of what is happening. The montage that comprises the practical component of a drama lesson, then, refers to the totality of all the actions in the lesson and it is assembled, as in any dramatic event, to produce specific effects.

In some lessons (particularly in early KS3) the pupils may be aware of following a story where the sequence of the lesson is tied to the stages of the story – beginning, middle and end – and which focuses on causal relationships between people, contexts and events in the story. In other lessons, the story may already be known or the source material for the lesson may not be in the form of a narrative. In such cases the structure of the dramatic montage is more visible. The various activities and tasks are assembled in such a way that pupils' attention is drawn to themes or ideas which develop and deepen as the work progresses but without being driven by a narrative logic. A tableau representing a particular moment in the story might be followed by pupils giving 'thoughts' to the characters in the tableau, or rearranging the figures in another group's tableau to demonstrate an alternative perspective – this sequence is designed to develop understanding of the human themes and issues without moving the narrative forward. The actions extend out from a moment suggested in the narrative, the lesson progresses in time, but the dramatic exploration is held to this moment in the narrative.

In most forms of drama the montage is notated, or recorded, as a sequence of **scenic units.** These units may correspond to the playwright's own division of the play into scenes. They may also correspond to the director's, or actors', division of the play into units which correspond to the development in the actors' performance or the emotional rhythms of the play. The study of the different ways in which theatre practitioners have and do construct montage, and the relationships between different genres of theatre (comedy, tragedy) and different approaches to montage, will be the focus in drama for pupils in KS4 and beyond.

However the montage is made, the scenic units must have meaning in themselves and also contribute to the complex meaning of the play as a whole. In other words, each unit must have its own logic for performers and audience, but also contribute to the logic of the whole performance. The concept of 'episode' is a useful construct for pupils to understand. They will know, from their experience of TV drama, that an episode of a TV series should make sense in itself but they also know that their understanding of characters and the 'meanings' the producers want to communicate accumulate over a number of episodes. So there is the sense of the episode both having its own shape and logic but also contributing to a developing understanding, which will only be complete when all the episodes have been watched.

Each scenic unit or episode of the montage provides a 3-dimensional experience for actors and audiences – it is not made of a single action such as a change in space or a line spoken, it is a complex of simultaneous actions that together offer meaning.

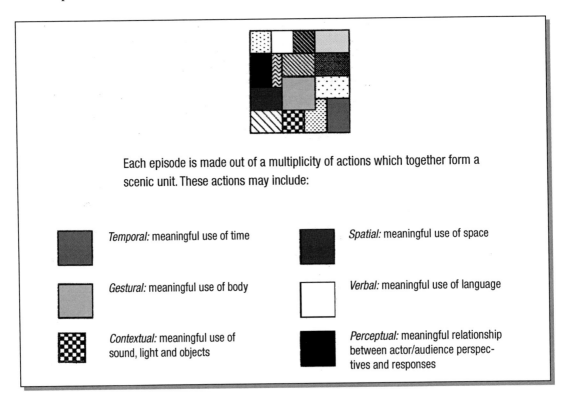

Each episode is made out of a multiplicity of actions which together form a scenic unit. These actions may include:

Temporal: meaningful use of time

Spatial: meaningful use of space

Gestural: meaningful use of body

Verbal: meaningful use of language

Contextual: meaningful use of sound, light and objects

Perceptual: meaningful relationship between actor/audience perspectives and responses

In drama education the division into scenic units may correspond to the exercises, tasks or improvisations that together constitute the lesson. The lesson plans in the next section of this book have been organised in such a way. The complete lesson plan represents the instructions for the montage as a whole but it is subdivided into units which, in my mind at least, make sense in themselves while also contributing to the pupils' progressive understanding of the themes and ideas in the drama as it unfolds and moves from one unit to the next.

In most forms of drama there is a specific requirement that each scenic unit will be played in the dramatic present. The dramatic present refers to the particular quality of time in drama. We appear to be producing, or witnessing, a 'here-and-now' representation in which events unfold as we see them – they are not reported past events as they are in story. But, in effect, the 'here-and-now' of drama must be linked to what has already happened or what we already know prior to this moment in the performance. The 'here-and-now' of drama must also imply a future or cause an audience to question how the events we are witnessing now will create future events. It is this sense of an implied future (or destiny), which is connected to past events through what is revealed in the events that are happening now on stage, that differentiates the dramatic present from the 'here-and-now' of everyday life. The present in drama is always in the margins between a tangible past and future.

The linking between the past and an implied future in each passing moment of the drama causes the audience to extend and deepen their understanding of the play's theme. Each passing moment should build on and clarify what has happened and clarify, through implication, our expectations of what will happen next.

In the diagram below, the boxes represent the episodes, scenic units or other divisions in the drama. The boxes are linked by the narrative, or thematic, thread that guides us through the drama. The arrows indicate the way in which the audience's understanding of the play's themes extends and expands as the drama progresses. Each scene implies the future while extending, confirming or confounding what has previously been revealed or implied.

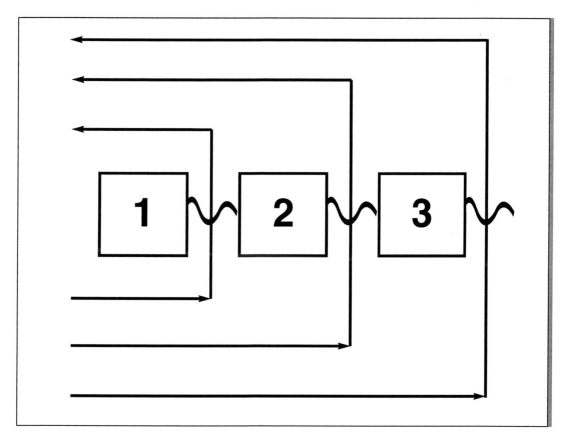

There may be further aesthetic considerations in making the montage. The relationship between scenic units may be used to create different kinds of rhythm. The **rhythm** of a drama may be tied to an emotional score – a balance of 'highs and lows' – or to the tensions in the relationships and events that are being represented. The rhythm in school drama, as in some forms of theatre, may create a balance between **efficacy** (where the purpose of the drama is to bring about some kind of change in understanding and attitude or to create lasting results for the participants) and **entertainment** (where pleasure and fun are given precedence).

The use of the elements of drama (time, space, people, objects, sound and light), the structuring concepts of 'montage' and scenic 'units', and the principles of playing a 'dramatic present' are common to both conventional theatre presentation and to curriculum drama at KS3. However, the drama teacher has additional concerns that guide the structuring of curriculum drama and which, inevitably, make such drama appear 'different' from some other forms of non-school theatre. These considerations include the following.

Working positively with the constraints of time, space and numbers

Drama is a very flexible art form but, even so, drama teachers often work with constraints that are quite unique to the school situation. The time allowed may vary from regular weekly slots between 45 minutes and an hour or more in length to shorter and/or less frequent periods. It is difficult in such circumstances to maintain the progressive experience of a montage. The time constraints may mean that pupils are forced to engage and work with drama more quickly and sketchily than in other forms of non-school drama. The spaces that are used for drama may vary from custom-built studios to corridors! The drama teacher is also working with a large number of actors who can't be expected to be mere extras to the work of star individuals – they must all be offered a meaningful and varied experience of producing drama.

Managing the planned with the lived

We have noted that curriculum drama differs from other forms of drama in the sense that it is not 'by choice'. Engagement has to be negotiated. Structuring in curriculum drama must take the lived experience of pupils into account in terms of their inhibitions, differing abilities, peer-group dynamics. The need to deliver a planned curriculum in drama that is related to the school curriculum and ethos as a whole is also a constraint on structuring. The teacher does not have a free rein. She is responsible for ensuring that lessons are productive, well ordered and supportive of the school's ethos. There is often a greater emphasis on the efficacious uses of drama (to produce specific results) than on providing entertainment (as important as the experience of pure pleasure in the theatre is).

Working with two aesthetic traditions

The principles and concepts of structuring that we have discussed are derived from the restricted art of literary theatre. They describe the way in which practitioners in conventional, 'serious', theatre approach their work. But, as we have noted, most pupils' aesthetic experience and knowledge is derived from the oral and communal aesthetic of film, TV and other forms of popular entertainment. Structuring in drama should not alienate pupils from their own cultural knowledge and practice – it should seek to build bridges between aesthetic traditions.

The principles that follow may help you to positively address these considerations – which are particular to the local context of making, performing and responding to drama within the curriculum.

Teach structuring through the experience of structure

Make the montage – the assembly of form and content – visible to pupils; discuss the choices that are being made; encourage pupils to use, and reflect on the use of, the full range of drama elements so that their own group work is three-dimensional.

Co-author to create co-ownership

Encourage suggestions about how to develop both the plot and the montage of the drama; work with and from the pupils' questions about the themes and ideas that are being dramatised. Use (and therefore pass on) your own skills and knowledge to enhance pupils' work – sound, lights, choreography and direction, where appropriate.

Introduce and use a diversity of conventions and traditions

Introduce and blend together conventions from other cultures and from film/TV. Avoid suggesting that there is a hierarchy of conventions in which the conventions of Western theatre have a 'natural' superiority over other traditions.

Prohibit unacceptable images

Art in school is restricted to representations and messages which are acceptable to the whole school community – pupil-artists are not free from censorship. Have no concerns about either banning, or confounding, prejudicial images and characterisations.

Use an episodic structure

This needs to be open-ended like the episodes of a TV series; each episode speaks for itself. Don't be tied to having to finish the story or to complete all the stages of a planned sequence. An episodic structure gives greater flexibility – you can extend or shorten the sequence of episodes according to the needs and interests of the group. Episodic structures are a familiar means of bridging the time gap between one episode and the next: see TV series, soaps, etc.

Use group work to cover more ground

Whenever possible give groups *different* tasks or scenes to do in order to cover more ground; stress difference; make watching more interesting. Encourage groups towards diversity of meaning rather than conformity. In terms of the response to group work, encourage pupils to extend their sense of 'possible meanings' rather than to reproduce the same ideas.

Stress the communal rather than the individual, and structure accordingly

Draw attention to the means and meanings used in group work rather than to comments about individual contributions and skill levels. Structure for ensemble work rather than principal characters – think of groups of characters rather than individuals. Run group presentations as a single performance sequence so that reflection is on the *whole* experience created by the group as a whole.

Practical drama work in schools often takes on a conventional structural shape **(genre)**. For instance, when I was trained to teach drama the genre we were given followed a conventional pattern of games/ice-breakers, short improvisations or scenes, followed by de-briefing and relaxation exercises. Whatever the content or objective for the lesson, we would try and fit what we were doing into this pattern. Nowadays there is a greater variety of genres of practical drama to be found – greater variety means greater choice for teachers and pupils. In the table that follows I have tried to identify some common genres of drama work and to offer some advice on structuring within each genre. I have tried to avoid creating a hierarchy of genres by giving greater value to some rather than others. It is my belief that all of these genres are needed in order to effectively deliver the practical component of the KS3 drama curriculum. I have, however, given extra consideration to the **conventions approach** because it is the genre that works best for me and I believe it to be particularly appropriate to KS3.

small group play making	*Pupils prepare their own scenes based on a title or theme. The work is performed to the other groups.*
	■ Break the production process of the scene into stages (beginning, middle and end, for instance) and give instruction and feedback at each stage
	■ Give opportunities for reworking scenes after feedback
	■ Focus on helping groups to clarify *what* is being communicated and *how* it might be communicated more effectively
	■ Encourage pupils to explore non-naturalistic conventions in their work, e.g. dance, masks, narration
rehearsal	*Pupils work on extracts or whole plays and are given responsibility for a full realisation, or performance, of the playwright's work. Through a process of rehearsal, pupils are expected to explore the meanings communicated by the playwright and how to codify those ideas in theatre form.*
	■ Encourage creative approaches to rehearsal by using other drama conventions such as improvisation, sculpting, 'tableau' or 'hot-seating' to research character, setting and language
	■ Don't leave it to the pupils – they need direction and knowledge from you. The pupils rely on you to make sure the finished work will not embarrass them!
	■ Be flexible with casting, use multiple characters or double-up or have different actors for different scenes
	■ Encourage pupils to use the full range of the elements of drama – light, space, objects – to comment on, or reinforce, the verbal playing of the text

skills development	*A particular skill, such as movement, voice, dance, mask-work or improvisation, is isolated and taught to pupils, who then practise in order to improve their expertise. Practising may involve following the teacher/trainer, private or group practice and applying the skill in a short game or exercise.*

- Establish the relevance of the skill to the drama work; how pupils will use it, how the training will help them to do better drama
- To feel comfortable in a skills-based exercise (such as learning to move in a mask so that the mask is always facing the audience), pupils may still need some sense of context and content. Drama is a concrete art in which players need a sense of real-life motive and purpose
- Use the pupils' strengths, focus on skills of agility, speed, dexterity and imaginative response – but avoid the fear of physical embarrassment!
- Use popular cultural forms as vehicles for skills development: rap, juggling, acrobatics, dance, ball games

living through	*Pupils, working with the teacher-in-role (a player in the drama), place themselves in an imagined situation and then, through making and taking characters, they behave as if they are living through the Imagined experience as it unfolds. How they act and react is determined both by the 'culture', or given circumstances, of the situation and also by agreed narrative characteristics such as elements of fantasy or an intensifying of the potential 'drama' of the situation.*

This is a very action-orientated genre. Quite literally, nothing will happen unless the participants take action themselves. In this way pupils are very conscious of forging their own histories through their actions, just as Shakespeare's characters were.

The development of this genre of theatre experience is closely associated with the work of Dorothy Heathcote and Gavin Bolton, but 'teacher-in-role' is also linked to the 'joker' in Augusto Boal's 'forum theatre' and to the old tradition of adults joining in and enhancing children's fantasy play. This genre is often used as a model for drama in KS1/2.

- Spend time constructing the context of the imagined situation – the 'W' questions
- Use teacher-in-role to initiate, model, guide and control the pupils' behaviour; weave together the pupils' responses; build atmosphere; work as a storyteller within the story
- Encourage pupils to create and try roles and role responses that are different from their own daily roles and behaviours

	■ Break the work up and include reflection, exercises and other conventions in the montage so that both the theatre and the analysis of behaviour offered by the imagined experience is not forgotten
conventions approach	*A 'laboratory theatre' approach in which some aspect of human behaviour or experience is isolated and selected for close exploration. The aspect may be contained in a playscript, a literary source or any text that comments on human nature/culture. The montage is made of episodes in which pupils use a variety of techniques or conventions to illuminate the content. An initial tableau of events may be followed by hot-seating characters or providing inner monologues for the initial tableau. The techniques used are derived from conventions which are local to curriculum drama – teacher-in-role, as well as from post-naturalist theatres – alter-egos, Brechtian devices, forum theatre.*

■ There must be an aesthetic logic to the montage: it's not enough to simply use a bag of different techniques – taken together the various exercises and techniques used must develop into a complete and satisfying dramatic experience
■ Look for opportunities to layer the work by combining conventions or reusing earlier work. We might provide the soundtrack of memories for a poignant moment that is caught in tableau, or repeat lines spoken earlier as we watch characters react to hearing them again
■ Don't move too rapidly from the use of one convention to another. Look for opportunities to use new conventions to further develop or investigate the pupils' work; rearrange the spatial relationships in a tableau, for instance, to see how the meaning changes, or, focus on a particular action or gesture and isolate it for discussion or as the basis for further creative extension

Knowledge

This will be the shortest of the sections, even though it ought to be the longest! It isn't possible to 'give' the knowledge that a drama teacher needs in these few pages. I am restricting myself to describing the different categories of knowledge and giving some sense of what might be included in each. (I have included only knowledge that is specific to drama teaching – not the basic body of pedagogic knowledge that all teachers need to acquire). Part of my own pleasure in teaching drama is knowing that I will never know enough – I need to constantly seek new knowledge that will enhance my practice. The breadth of knowledge that I describe here will take experience and time to gain. The knowledge is to be found through reading the books suggested in the annotated bibliography and beyond. It is to be found through going to the theatre and cinema as often as possible and through going to workshops. It is also to be found through experience, both of teaching drama and of being attentive to the world around us.

In order to be an effective subject specialist in drama at KS3, a teacher needs to acquire knowledge in these five categories: *practical, theoretical, technical, historical, cultural.* There will of course be overlap between these categories – masks are placed in practical knowledge because there are traditions and particular uses of masks that teachers should know about, but technical knowledge is needed in order to teach mask-making.

At first glance the knowledge that is described may seem to go far beyond the requirements of the KS3 curriculum. Certainly, you don't need everything that is here to be a drama teacher at KS3. But the more knowledge you have of drama yourself the more you have to draw on and inform your teaching at any key stage. In the English educational system, a drama specialist is required to have knowledge equivalent at least to A-level.

Practical knowledge

- dramaturgy; the use of the elements of drama to communicate meanings
- acting styles, dance, masks and other relevant aspects of stage craft
- management of personal and interpersonal behaviour
- project management (production).

Theoretical knowledge

- specific to teaching drama in schools (books like this one, for instance)
- dramatic theory (which might range from the works of Aristotle to Raymond Williams and the theoretical writings of Brecht, Stanislavski and others)
- semiotics of drama (how meanings in theatre are constructed, communicated and reconstructed by audiences)
- theatre anthropology (the different cultural uses and manifestations of performances in other times and places as well as our own)
- the theoretical writing of key twentieth and twenty-first century theatre and school drama practitioners (which might include Slade, Way, Heathcote and Bolton but also Stanislavski, Meyerhold, Brecht and Boal)
- awareness of relevant critical theory – feminist, post-colonialist, performance, literary.

Technical knowledge

- sound and light technology
- use of IT as a control system for the above and for use as part of drama (using the World Wide Web for research, for instance)
- scenic design and construction (including costumes and properties).

Historical knowledge

- major periods and styles of Western theatre – Greek, Elizabethan/Jacobean, Realism/Naturalism, Symbolism and Expressionism
- twentieth century and pre-twentieth century playwrights, e.g. Shakespeare, Jonson, Brecht, Miller
- genres of tragedy and comedy
- key periods of social history – e.g. Athenian and Elizabethan societies, Industrial Revolution, 1930s and 1960s
- popular theatres and entertainment, e.g. mysteries, commedia, melodrama, vaudeville, federal theatre projects, musicals.

Cultural knowledge

- major non-European performance traditions, e.g. Kathakali, Noh and Kabuki, Carnival, shadow puppets
- contemporary trends in writing and performance styles
- media and representation
- major cultural movements such as modernism and postmodernism
- the oral and communal aesthetic tradition.

3

Resources

Year 7 – Introducing Antigone

Rationale

This introduction to Sophocles' *Antigone* provides opportunities for developing a wide range of skills, knowledge and understanding about drama. The play itself is among the most accessible of the Athenian tragedies and gives an introduction to the classic structure of tragedy, including the role of the chorus and the unities of time, place and plot. *Antigone* is also a powerful myth in its own right and its themes of the collisions between public and private lives, tensions between family and civic loyalties and between generations have a contemporary appeal for younger pupils. There is also a strong appeal in Antigone herself, who is a feisty 13-year-old prepared to die for what she believes in her heart to be true. This sequence of lessons combines exploration of the myth through a variety of drama conventions and techniques, with an introduction to fragments of the translated text and the form and structure of Athenian tragedy.

Resources

Three hours of class time and one homework
Large sheets of paper and markers
Copy(ies) of Jean Cocteau's drawing
The Thebans by Sophocles, translated by Timberlake Wertenbaker (Faber & Faber 1992)
Extracts from the script

Specialist and framework objectives

Specialist Learning Strand objectives: Acting/Inter-acting	A1: use and control the elements of drama, particularly voice and the body in space
	A2: use voice, gesture and movement to convey meaning to an audience, making disciplined use of the conventions of performance
	AI1: work as part of an ensemble – acting and reacting to others

Directing/Managing	D5: translate initial ideas and responses into drama
	M1: learn to negotiate with others in a group and to adapt to and accommodate other people's ideas
Evaluating/Reviewing	R1: identify historical and current genres of drama, e.g. tragedy
	E2: develop critical thinking about texts, issues and situations through work in role
Framework objectives: **Drama**	SL15: explore in role
	SL17: extend their spoken repertoire
S&L	SL11: adopt a range of roles in discussion
	SL13: work together logically and methodically to solve problems, make deductions
Reading	TR6: adopt active reading approaches
	TR7: identify the main points, processes or ideas in a text
	TR12: comment on how writers convey setting, character and mood
	TR18: give a considered response to a play
	TR20: explore the notions of literary heritage … why some texts have been particularly influential or significant

Selected specialist teaching approaches

- Create a protective environment for pupils to experiment with their voices and movement without self-consciousness.

- Use a variety of techniques and conventions to explore character, settings and plot though drama rather than through discussion.

- Demonstrate, and then provide opportunities for pupils to take on roles, particularly adult roles that require them to imagine themselves differently.

- Teach pupils how to represent characters in context in 'here and now' situations, using visual, aural, linguistic, spatial and physical signs to convey a 'living reality' for an audience.

- Model ways of communicating character through a range of techniques, including teacher-in-role, tableaux, hot-seating.

- Direct examples of group work to demonstrate how to communicate ideas to an audience through dramatic techniques and conventions of staging.

- Encourage less confident pupils to take on powerful roles in the drama and create situations where pupils need to solve problems through appropriate dialects and registers.

- Identify and use examples of good work as models for other groups to follow.

- Compare different dramatic interpretations of a scene so that pupils become aware of the variety of possibilities.

- Model activities which challenge the pupils and demand co-operation and negotiation in paired and small group work.

- Create opportunities for critical reflection so that pupils think about and articulate their insights from the drama experience.

- Ensure that lessons have reflection and evaluation as learning objectives from the outset.

Performance indicators

During the sequence of lessons, pupils always/sometimes/rarely:

- work effectively and co-operatively with others both in an out of role;

- use voice and movement to convey character, matching dialect and register to role and situation;

- contribute ideas to discussion, listening to and incorporating the ideas of others;

- analyse dialogue in scripts and other texts and form ideas about characters;

- observe and maintain social rules for class discussion and group work;

- recognise and comment on the dramatic potential of the given circumstances;

- use critical questioning to develop and refine ideas;

- comment positively and critically on their own work and that of others;

- recognise and can discuss relationships between form, content and intention in scripts, texts and dramas created;

- reflect, during devising, rehearsal and discussion, on relevant themes, ideas and issues.

Context for the story

Antigone (442–41 BC) was the first of a trilogy of plays that Sophocles wrote to tell the tragic story of the royal house of Thebes. At the heart of this story is the tragedy of Oedipus. Oedipus was brought up by foster-parents and set out on a journey to find his natural parents. Through a disastrous series of unwitting mistakes, Oedipus kills a stranger in an angry quarrel only to discover, much later, that the stranger was, in fact, his father, King Laius of Thebes. He also marries the widow Jocasta, who bears him two sons and two daughters. Then he discovers that Jocasta is his natural mother. As a result of this shame, Jocasta kills herself and Oedipus blinds himself and goes into exile. Eventually he 'dies' in mysterious circumstances.

Oedipus passes over control of Thebes to Jocasta's brother Creon, but his sons, Polynices and Eteocles, will not accept this decision and both make rival challenges to Creon's power. Eventually, Polynices joins forces with the city of Argos, the enemies of Thebes, and invades. Despite his differences with Creon, Eteocles bravely defends Thebes against his brother's attack and both end up killing each other.

In order to deter any further treason and to bring order back to Thebes, Creon decrees that Eteocles should be buried with full honours while his brother's body must be left to rot outside the city gates. Anyone who tries to bury Polynices shall be stoned to death. The Greeks believed it to be vital for a body to be properly buried and taken to the 'underworld' below. It was the responsibility of the family to ensure that there was a proper burial ritual. The story of *Antigone* begins with the Prologue in which Oedipus' two daughters, Antigone and Ismene, discuss Creon's decree.

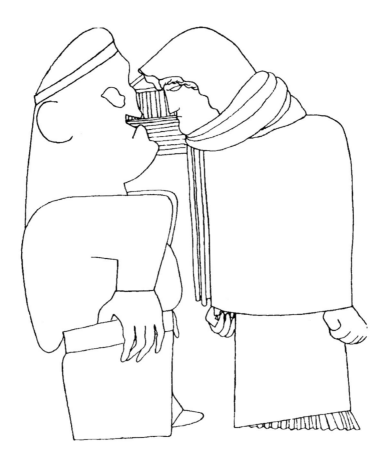

Teaching Episode 1 Establishing themes and relevance

Teacher projects Jean Cocteau's 1922 drawing of *Antigone et Creon* and asks class to discuss with their neighbours: 'Who do you think is the taller of these two characters?'

Teacher guides class discussion of responses, noting how the pupils give 'character' to the two figures. How can they tell it's a man/woman? What can they tell about the relationship or conflict between the two figures from the drawing? What time and/or culture does the drawing represent?

The drawing is a simple and non-threatening visual introduction to the play for young pupils. In the drawing Cocteau captures many of the play's themes:

- the conflict of will and ideologies between Antigone and Creon;
- the importance of generation and gender to that conflict;
- the struggle for power between Antigone and Creon;
- Creon's fear that he will become a woman if he loses the conflict;
- the gendering of concepts of power, family and responsibility; and
- the clash between public and family duties and roles.

Teacher tells the class that the drawing is of two of the characters in a very old play from fifth century BCE Athens called *Antigone*. Antigone is the female figure and Creon (or Kreon) is the male. Creon is Antigone's uncle and also king of the city they both live in. The city is called Thebes. Teacher asks the class to use this information to discuss with their neighbours ideas about potential characters, settings and plots in the play.

Teacher lays out four large pieces of paper around the space; each piece has a line from the text written on it:

1. *I am no longer the man, she is the man . . .*
   As long as I live I shall not be ruled by women
2. *We must remember we are born women and are not meant to do battle against men*
3. *There is nothing shameful when a man, even a wise man, learns something*
4. *The sorrows of the living pile on the sorrows of the dead*

Teacher invites the class to read and think about each of these lines and then decide which makes them either the angriest or which they agree the most with. When they have decided, pupils move to the appropriate sheet of paper and discuss their reasons with others who have made the same choices. Teacher invites each group to share their thoughts and feelings with the class and asks, in each case, whether people still think like that or say similar things.

Teacher uses the convention of the *five-second tableau*, in which the group only has five seconds to negotiate and physically make an image together. The first tableau is of their chosen line from a man's perspective and then a second tableau is made from a woman's perspective. Groups discuss what they made and how it changed from one tableau to the next, and then share with the class.

This exercise serves a number of teaching and learning purposes:

- The lines illustrate important themes in the play so that pupils will begin their exploration of the plot with these themes in mind – working at theme level rather than plot level.

- The teacher invites an emotional response from pupils and encourages them to discuss their responses together in public – in this way the class are modelling the idea of 'chorus' and also of the Athenian public debates in the *agora* or market place about topical issues.

- Among the topical issues when *Antigone* was first performed were issues related to democracy and dictatorship. Athens, a democracy, was at war with Sparta, a dictatorship. There was also continuing debate about the role of women in public life – despite democracy, women and others were excluded. Another issue was related to a growing number of 'wild girls', or 'bears' (*arktoi*) as the Athenians called them, who were challenging the authority of parents and elders and running wild in the streets late at night.

- All of these themes can be demonstrated to be relevant today for young people, and establishing Antigone as a 12/13-year-old girl who is prepared to die for what her heart feels to be true makes her appealing and relevant to Year 7 pupils. These themes may also be very differently understood in multicultural classrooms where careful guiding of discussion will model citizenship which respects and tries to understand difference.

- The five-second tableaux offer pupils an alternative physical and silent means of 'dialogue' about their interpretations of the lines. They only have time to follow their instincts and to try and feel what others in the group are trying to do. Reflecting on instinctive physical and emotional responses to a given cue is part of learning to act.

Teacher guides a plenary reflection on what the class have learnt about *Antigone* so far, and ties together and makes a note of the important contributions from the discussions during the episode.

Rather than beginning with the text or plot, this first episode begins with exercises that model the social and cultural function of tragedy in fifth-century BCE Athens as a mirror of society and as a means of provoking debate and dialogue amongst citizens. The exercises also introduce the class to the idea of the chorus representing the citizens and their views.

Episode 2 From text to performance

Teacher explains that the class will work like 'detectives' to try and piece together Antigone's story.

> The objective is to let the pupils 'discover' the story through exploring fragments of text rather than to give a lengthy exposition, which might both bore them and put them off further study of the play and Athenian drama in general. Pupils need to feel comfortable with not knowing the whole picture as they begin work on the extracts.

To begin with, the teacher gives out two extracts from the Prologue; Antigone's and Ismene's speeches. The teacher explains that a prologue comes at the beginning of a play and that the beginnings of plays often also tell us about the past (the *backstory*) and what will come later, as well as establishing the 'here and now' of the play. Teacher introduces the term *exposition* for this playwrighting process.

The speeches are divided into numbered sections and the teacher divides the class up into either six or 12 groups depending on ability and size of class. If six, then each group takes one of the sections from each sister's speeches so that they have two sections to work with. If 12, then each group has just one section. Each section has annotated notes to help the pupils.

> These annotations may need to be in more detail according to ability; but they should only help pupils to understand their section – there is no need to tell the whole story yet.

ANTIGONE:

1. We have two brothers. Hasn't Creon honoured one with a tomb and shamed the other? *[Creon is the ruler of Thebes; the two brothers of Antigone are also his nephews]*

2. Eteocles, they say, has been buried, with due observance of justice and custom, under the ground, to be honoured among the dead. *[Eteocles is one of the brothers; the Greeks believed that bodies must be properly buried]*

3. As for Polynices, they say it is forbidden by decree to bury him, or mourn him, but he is to be left unwept, unburied, a sweet morsel for the birds as they look down – their treasure-store of tasty meat. *[Polynices is the other brother who betrayed Thebes and attacked the city and his brother and uncle Creon]*

4. That is the good Creon's proclamation to you and to me – yes, to me – and he is coming here to make this clear to those who may still not know. And this is no small matter. *[Creon has ordered that Polynices's body must be left to rot without being buried]*

5. Whoever does these things anyway will be stoned in front of the people of the city. *[Creon has ordered that anyone who tries to bury Polynices will be stoned to death in public]*

6. That's how it is for you as well and you will soon show whether you are well born or the bad shoot of good stock. *[Antigone and her sister Ismene are also banned and Antigone wonders whether Ismene will do her duty and bury her brother, or is she too scared?]*

ISMENE:

1. Oimoi,
   Think,
   sister
   how our father died –
   hated, in shame
   shunned
   uncovering himself his own guilt and striking his two eyes with his own hands. *[The sister's father was Oedipus who died in shame after taking out his own eyes]*

2. And then the mother, wife, double name, mangling her life in that tangle of ropes. *[The sisters' mother was Oedipus' wife, but she discovered she was also Oedipus' mother so she strangled herself]*

3. And finally, our two brothers, in one day each miserably slaying the other, trapped in a shared fate wreaked by their own hands. *[The two brothers killed each other in the battle of Thebes]*

4. We are the two left behind. Alone. We too will die most miserably if we violate the decree and defy the power of the tyrant. *[Creon has ordered that one of the brothers, Polynices, must not be buried. Anyone who tries will be stoned to death]*

5. We must remember we are born women and are not meant to do battle against men. And then that we are ruled by those who are the stronger and we must obey this and things even more painful.

6. And so I beg forgiveness of those below, I am compelled: I have to obey those in power. There is no sense in the excessive gesture. *[Ismene asks forgiveness from her ancestors because she will not break the law by trying to bury her brother Polynices]*

Teacher scaffolds the group's work towards physicalising and visualising their sections:

- Each group is given their section to read among themselves and begin to discuss clues to the story. They list any words they don't understand and the teacher collects these words and, with the class, offers definitions of their meaning. Then each group reads out their section around the class until all twelve have been shared.

- Teacher explains that pupils will work on using their voices in interesting ways to 'perform' their section. The teacher models choices for the class – one voice, chorus, overlapping voices, echoes, repetition etc.

- Pupils work on vocalising their section (they must use the given text). When they are ready, teacher asks them to work on a tableau to illustrate their section effectively.

- When the group has had time to prepare their tableau, the teacher asks them to find a creative way of moving togther into the tableau while also vocalising the text. This work also involves thinking about where in the space each group wants to begin and end their movement into the still image.

– When all the groups are ready, the teacher directs a class performance with each group following on from the next without a break.

> This is a 'performance' which needs careful managing so that the class experience the full dramatic effect of their work – they need to create but also experience the work. Make sure the space is organised effectively and that groups are clear about the order and the need to begin and end in stillness as a signal to the next group to begin.

Teacher leads whole-class reflection on the qualities of each group's work and the overall effect of the performance as a whole. Teacher uses the four quotes used in the first teaching episode to prompt class to discuss themes emerging from the play and to piece together what they now know about the backstory and plot.

Episode 3 Creating context and relevance

Teacher asks class to imagine what life in Thebes might be like. This is a city recovering from a war and siege by enemies led by Polynices. Comparisons are made with Baghdad or with any other city torn with conflict. In pairs, pupils discuss what their priorities would be if they were put in charge of a city like Baghdad. How would they establish law and order? How would they protect the people from further attacks? How would they make sure their authority was respected? What would be the differences between ruling the city in a time of war as opposed to in peacetime?

> The comparisons with Baghdad and postwar Iraq offer an opportunity to create a strong sense of historical relevance, and the televised events of the war and its aftermath may help pupils to begin to understand Creon's dilemma as a ruler. It is important for the pupils to understand and empathise with Creon's need to assert his authority as ruler in order to bring peace to Thebes.

Teacher asks class what kinds of people might travel to a city like Baghdad/Thebes immediately after war. Class make suggestions which might include: relatives looking for their families; aid and charity workers; journalists (messengers from other cities) seeking news stories; opportunists looking to make money; mercenaries; spies.

Teacher then establishes a whole-group role play with the teacher-in-role in the following ways:

1. Teacher uses two chairs or similar to mark out one of the 'seven gates of Thebes'. Teacher tells the class that it is dawn on the first day since the enemies of Thebes retreated from the city walls. The gates are locked from the inside and will not be opened to outsiders until the city is ready for visitors. The teacher lays out the four sheets of paper used for the quotes exercise in the shape of a body and tells the class that: *'Here lies the body of Polynices, a son of Thebes, turned traitor and now dead; killed by his own brother in battle.'*

2. Teacher asks pupils to individually decide which of the roles they want to adopt from the suggestions made earlier. As the pupils decide, the teacher explains that they are a group of travellers waiting for the gates to be opened. Teacher invites the class to gather together and to start talking with the other 'travellers', sharing gossip and news about what has happened in Thebes. Once the class has begun to talk together and feels confident with being in role as travellers, the teacher interrupts to say: *'Close to the body of Polynices, sits a guard* [teacher in role]. *This is your chance to fill in the gaps in the story and to ask questions in your roles as travellers to Thebes that will help you to understand what's happening and what might happen next.'*

3. In role as the guard, the teacher approaches the class and uses some of the content and themes from the first chorus of *Antigone*, which includes reference to it being a beautiful morning, the enemies have departed after a terrible war, the people are tired of war and now want to celebrate and get back to normal.

> The class might return to this moment and look at the text of the first chorus and what it tells us about the attitudes of the other citizens of Thebes.

4. Teacher interacts with the class in role, inviting questions, filling in any gaps in the story, explaining why Polynices is to be left unburied, reminding the class that Polynices was a traitor and that the Thebans want a strong leader and to set an example to their enemies. Teacher develops the role play trying to encourage the class to take different viewpoints on the situation so that sympathies are divided between Antigone's desire to bury her brother and Creon's desire to make an example of Polynices in order to stop any further bloodshed and disturbance in the city.

> The teacher in role as the guard functions as 'information giver', fleshing out the details of the backstory, in particular the tragedy of Oedipus, and making sure the class can understand why Creon and many others in the city think that Polynices is a traitor who deserves to be left unburied as a deterrent.

5. Once the class is established in role and has usefully interrogated and interacted with the 'guard', the teacher stops the conversations and points into the distance saying: *'Sssh! Look here comes Antigone, the sister of dead Polynices; she hasn't heard the news yet! There's going to be some trouble now!'*. Teacher stops the role play and invites a volunteer to take on the role of Antigone.

> This is an important opportunity for a pupil to take on a central role and interact with the rest of the class. It may take some prompting from the teacher to get a volunteer. If no-one is willing, teacher can suggest that two pupils share the role or, as a last resort, the teacher can begin by modelling how Antigone might react to the chorus and guard and then ask a volunteer to take over the role. The teacher in the role of the guard has to manage the class so that Antigone gets a chance to speak and, as far as possible, she is answered by pupils rather than by the teacher. The teacher tries to create a sense of chorus by encouraging different points of view on Antigone's situation and dilemma.

6. Teacher in role as the guard facilitates and manages, in role, the interaction between the pupil who has taken on the role of Antigone and the crowd. As far as possible, the teacher tries to get the 'chorus' of travellers to put different points of view to Antigone and to try and persuade her not to risk her life by disobeying Creon. At an appropriate point, the guard announces that the gates are now open and the travellers can now enter. Teacher then stops the role play and asks which of the travellers would now enter the city and go about their own business and which would want to stay and see what happens to Antigone. Out of role, the pupils discuss and reflect on their choices and reasons for either staying or going.

> The tension here is designed to encourage the pupils to think about private and public responsibilities – do they think it more important to go on about their own private business, looking for lost relatives for instance, or to stay and try and see that justice is done for Antigone.

Episode 4 Discovering the tragic

The class is divided into four groups and given the following tasks and instructions. '*What if Antigone had all the time in the world to think about what she might say to the guard? What would she say? What if she had all the time in the world to think about what to say to the travellers? To Creon? To the Gods? What would she say?*'

Each group is given responsibility for discussing and deciding on Antigone's words to either the guard, travellers, Creon or the Gods. Each group must choose an 'Antigone' to play the role and speak the words.

> The whole-group role play required pupils to think on their feet and to make fairly instinctive responses to the situation as it unfolds. It is important now to slow the pace of the work so that pupils can be more critically aware of what is happening and also to encourage them to be highly selective in their use of language in order to mirror the hightened language and 'literariness' of the text itself. In this way the pupils begin by exploring the situation through the oral and communal aesthetic of whole-class improvisation and then move to the more considered and crafted use of language and gesture associated with the literary and private aesthetic tradition.

When they are ready, the teacher explains that there were three different kinds of movement/gesture used by actors in Athenian tragedy and models possible examples that Antigone might use at this point:

- *index*, or pointing towards other characters or places;
- *icon*, or mimetic gestures such as covering the face for crying or shaking a fist to show anger; and
- *schema*, or more symbolic gestures which try to convey ideas or concepts – such as family, or loyalty, or loss.

Each group must now decide on an appropriate gesture for their Antigone when she speaks.

When the groups have prepared their Antigones, the teacher asks the four pupils who are chosen to act Antigone to meet together and decide in which order they should speak and do their gestures, and where in the space each should stand. Meanwhile, the teacher works with the rest of the class, asking them in pairs to think about what their role might want to say to Antigone and what gesture they will choose to use.

When the class is ready, the teacher directs by signalling to the Antigones to come and speak their lines and then stay in the space like a statue until all four are in place. Then each of the pupils in the 'chorus' of travellers speaks their line to Antigone and makes their gesture one after another.

The exercise is then repeated, but this time the pupils only make their gesture – they do not speak. The teacher encourages them to think about how to make their silent gestures more powerful and expressive now that they have no words. The teacher plays an appropriately atmospheric piece of music as a soundtrack to this.

This is a conscious attempt to create a powerful and moving moment of theatre. Pupils should be encouraged to develop and extend their silent gestures in response to others and to the music being played. In a sense, this is a moment of 'catharsis', of releasing emotions and emotional energy through the making and experiencing of a strong theatre event.

Extensions

This scheme has provided a detailed description of a potential introduction to *Antigone*. The class might go on to:

★ hot-seat teacher-in-role as Creon about his motives and reasons for decreeing that Polynices body be left unburied;

★ explore the scenes between Creon and Haemon (Creon's son) and Creon and Antigone and consider the issues raised about love and loyalty, both to one's family and to the state;

★ role play an imagined scene between Antigone and Haemon, perhaps using *collective voices* to create the dialogue between them as Antigone explains her decision and Haemon reacts to her;

★ explore the final scene and use a variety of techiniques to reflect on the characters and their contribution to the tragedy and to project how these events will shape Creon's and Thebes's futures;

★ meet as the citizens of Thebes to reflect on the events of the play and what they should learn from them for the future; and

★ discuss and critically reflect on the tensions between family and civic duty, the role of leaders and citizens.

Year 8 – Devising process based on a text stimulus

Rationale

Devising scripted and unscripted performances is a key skill required for GCSE which should be developed during Key Stage 3. This scheme of work challenges pupils to use their collective imaginings, based on a short text stimulus to create a polished performance with fully developed characters and relationships. The scheme provides a clear sense of structure to assist the scaffolding of the pupils' responses into a collective but coherent shared performance. The scheme also encourages pupils to consider the relationship between character and environment, which is a key understanding in the study of realist genres of theatre, familiar to pupils from TV and film.

Resources

Three hours of class time and one homework
Large sheets of paper and markers
Copies of the text extract
OHP transparencies and pens
OHP and screen

Specialist and framework objectives

Specialist Learning Strand objectives: Acting/Inter-Acting	A4: play a wide range of characters in different styles, based on research, observation and personal interpretation IA4: contribute ideas and establish productive working relationships
Directing/Managing	D4: direct the work of writers, actors and designers into a coherent dramatic statement M1: learn to negotiate with others in a group M4: suggest ways of synthesising and integrating ideas offered in groups
Reviewing/Evaluating	R2: use a critical and specialist vocabulary for discussing drama E3: analyse and account for their responses to texts
Framework objectives: Drama	SL15: explore and develop ideas through work in role SL16: collaborate in, and evaluate, the presentation of performances which explore character relationships and issues

S&L	SL4: provide an explanation or commentary which links words with actions and images SL10: use talk to question, hypothesise, speculate, evaluate, solve problems and develop thinking about complex issues and ideas
Reading	TR16: recognise how texts refer to and reflect the culture in which they were produced TR8: investigate how meanings are changed when information is presented in different forms or transposed into different media
Writing	TW7: experiment with different language choices to imply meaning and to establish the tone of a piece

Selected specialist teaching approaches

- Use a variety of techniques and conventions to explore character, settings and plot though drama rather than through discussion.
- Teach pupils how to represent characters in context in 'here and now' situations, using visual, aural, linguistic, spatial and physical signs to convey a 'living reality' for an audience.
- Model ways of communicating character through a range of techniques, including teacher-in-role, tableaux, hot seating.
- Identify and use examples of good work as models for other groups to follow.
- Compare different dramatic interpretations of a scene so that pupils become aware of the variety of possibilities.
- Model activities which challenge the pupils and demand co-operation and negotiation in paired and small-group work.
- Ensure that lessons have reflection and evaluation as learning objectives from the outset.
- Make explicit use of targets related to achievement and specify the criteria that will be used for assessment.
- Provide pupils with the means of making visual explorations and presentations of ideas.
- Demonstrate and explore how lighting, props and staging can enhance the dramatic communication and realisation of ideas.

Performance indicators

During the sequence of lessons, pupils always/sometimes/rarely:

- recognise and discuss cultural, moral and social issues raised by characterisation and explorations in role;
- understand the written conventions of a dramatic script and different ways in which plays are structured;

- work constructively and collaboratively to plan and shape dramatic representations;
- reflect on the impact of a performance on an audience and how to modify / improve it; and
- identify issues in the work and find ways to focus the group on the exploration.

Stimulus

From the beginning of Godfrey Goodwin's *There Ain't No Angels No More* (1978, Collins):

Crack! The stone cools my ear, hits the bollard at the end of our road and spends itself against the boarded window of what had once been our corner shop. It was the Laz boys from the Row beyond the 'Engineer' again. They do not like our street. We do not like them either so I do not see why they should like us. Only, why they have to pick on me I do not know. I try to slip out of school and get home with as little trouble as possible. Mind you, I can throw a stone when I have to because it's no use being an angel when you live in hell and that is what the gangs round about our street call it – 'Hell's Alley'. But we call it home.

Teaching Episode 1 Initial responses and analysis of the 'given circumstances'

Teacher introduces the scheme of work and its objectives. The outcome of the scheme will be a devised performance based on a text stimulus. Teacher explains that devising means creating an original piece of drama for performance based on selecting and shaping ideas from the class's exploration of a stimulus or starting point. Teacher explains that this process requires us to reflect on and record our ideas and experiences in the exploratory phase and suggests ways that this will be done – drawings, fragments of script, role-on-the-wall, for instance. The need for groups to find effective ways of working together and the kind of group contract needed for such work is discussed and some general principles established and written down.

Teacher gives out copies of the text stimulus and asks a volunteer to read. In groups, pupils are asked to look for clues in the stimulus. Each group is given a large sheet of paper which they divide into three columns for *characters*, *settings* and *plot*. Using these headings, pupils are invited to speculate and hypothesise, based on what they imagine from the clues provided in the text.

Pupils enjoy working in 'detective' mode – looking closely in the text for clues. The teacher uses the headings of *character*, *setting* and *plot* in order to signal the differences between textual analysis in drama and English. Pupils will be used to word, sentence and text-level analysis and to looking at the structure of language and imagery, but the focus here is on identifying the dramatic material in the extract. Pupils' prior experience of textual analysis in English will be useful however. They may, for instance, pick up on the paradox between the contacted words and phrases in the title and the lack of familiar contractions in the narrator's speech. Is this to do with class, or because the narrator is speaking English as an additional language?

It is important for the teacher to signal to the class that they are free to imagine but they must base their ideas on something suggested in the text so that there is a clear link between what they imagine and what they know about characters, settings and plot suggested in the text.

Teacher leads class discussion of each group's ideas, modelling how to integrate or consider ideas which are very different. Teacher asks class to justify their 'imaginings' by referring back to triggers in the text.

This discussion needs careful management so that different ideas and interpretations are included and valued, while the teacher also steers the class to some degree of necessary consensus in order to ensure that this is a whole-class exploration. Some ambiguities can be left open for further exploration – the gender of the narrator, for instance. The teacher needs to use this as an opportunity for modelling how the same extract can be interpreted in different ways and this offers a rich pool of possibilities for the class to draw on during the devising process.

Teacher explains that the purpose of the work will be to create a drama based on the extract. Class discuss the differences between prose and dramatic narratives. The teacher focuses on the idea of dramatic tension and, if necessary, explains and gives examples of dramatic tension. Groups are then asked to list possible tensions in the extract, for instance between:

gang/cultural territories;

home and school;

outsider perceptions (*Hell's Alley*) of the neighbourhood and local perceptions (*we call it home*);

older residents and new or migrant residents;

tradition and change.

Episode 2   Creating the dramatic context

Teacher explains that the devising process will begin with the class's ideas about a set design for the play. Each group is asked to create a collective 'impression', on large sheets of paper, of how the stage might look based on their notes and imaginings in Episode 1. The groups are encouraged to think about how the possible tensions that have been discussed might be represented in the set design – the tension between territories for instance. They are also encouraged to focus on how the audience will be placed. Teacher models different possibilities for the audience – proscenium, in the round, three sides, promenade.

> This exercise can offer an opportunity to teach the vocabulary and basic techniques and templates for stage design, if appropriate. The intention here is to focus the class's attention on environment and to create an expressive visual impression. By beginning with a visualisation of the setting, pupils are more likely to consider the effect of the environment on the shaping of characters and events later in the devising process. The purpose is to introduce, through practical work, a key idea in realist genres of theatre, which is that characters and events are shaped and determined by their environments. This characteristic of realism is to be found in a wide range of plays, including works by Ibsen, Hauptmann, Shaw, O'Neill, D.H. Lawrence, O'Neill and Miller. If the exercise is also being used as an introduction to design, the teacher might introduce illustrations from previous school productions or from professional examples on the internet. Design constraints might also be introduced – a set budget, or only using materials available in the drama space, for instance. Groups could also discuss ways of overcoming technical problems in the realisation of their designs.

When the groups have finished their drafts, teacher provides each group with an OHT and OHT markers and asks them to transcribe their drawings ready for presentation to the class. Teacher introduces a frame for the presentation. The play is going to be produced by Cameron Mackintosh the theatre impressario, The class are groups of stage designers who will have to make a 'pitch' to CM for their design concept. Each group decides how best to present their ideas and who will speak for the group. Each group presents their ideas using the OHP to project a large image of their drawing for the rest of the class to see. After each presentation, the teacher selects pupils in role as CM's representatives to comment on positive features of the presentation and to make suggestions for further improvement.

> Projecting the images gives a larger scale to the drawing, which helps to give an 'impression' of how the stage might look and be used. Pupils present in a formal register using the OHP just as the teacher might, to explain and elaborate their visual ideas. Speaking up in public with clarity and confidence is an important social skill for pupils to develop. The frame gives a purpose, relevance and some self-distance and fun to the task.

Episode 3 The circle of life

Teacher introduces and explains the convention of *Circle of Life* which the class will use to create ideas about character and plot.

Description of the convention

A large sheet of paper is divided into five sections: a circle in the centre of the page where the name and age of a central character are written and the surrounding paper then divided into four sections that will represent areas of that character's life and the people they interact with at those times. These sections are labelled: Home; Family; Play; and Day.

The heading: 'Home' indicates where the character normally lives, while 'Family' indicates any immediate or extended family and may include estranged family members we might otherwise expect to find at home. 'Play' indicates any type of social life and, finally, 'Day' indicates the character's workplace, if appropriate, or otherwise encompasses their daily routine, for example, if they are too young to work or are unemployed.

These headings are, hopefully, as value-free as possible so that groups can determine for themselves the specifics of the entries to be made. The group then, collectively, suggests ideas about the character and these ideas are entered into the appropriate section. The teacher manages this exercise to try and include different possibilities and ideas, and encourages the class to find connections and coherence in the suggestions made.

Here is an example of some of the ideas generated by a Year 8 class who decided that the central character was the narrator – Marty Brown, aged 12. The class decided to keep the ambiguity of whether Marty was a boy or girl.

The group is then subdivided into four smaller groups, each of which takes responsibility for a different section and creates, through improvisation, a short dialogue between the central character and one other significant character selected from their chosen section of the diagram (friend, foe, ally, relative). This dialogue should introduce potential conflicts, tensions or character details. These improvised dialogues are initially based on the previous collective agreements.

HOME

No. 4 Hell's Alley (Acacia Terrace)

Lives at home with Mum

Sister, Mo

FAMILY

Brother, Pete, in the Army

Dad lives on the other side of town

Has a Gran and sees her at weekends

Marty Brown, aged 12

has best friend, Fred, a girl

Paper-round for *Quickie News*

Mr Sprogg, Headteacher

PLAY

Likes computer games and tries to stay away from the streets at night. Belongs to the Alley Cats gang, but only for protection against against the Laz boys.

DAY

Goes to school. Tries to stay out of trouble

Lawrence Welk, leader of the Laz Boys
Ms Samms, Class teacher

Episode 4   From improvisation to script

Group are given responsibility for deciding on the best way of creating the improvised dialogue. This might include breaking each group into pairs, pairs improvising and then sharing with the rest of the group, until a final polished version is agreed. Class might also decide to allocate roles of writers, directors and actors.

> This provides an opportunity for pupils to reflect on their own working processes and to take responsibility for the management of the task in ways that are inclusive of the whole group and their strengths. Groups might use this as an assessment opportunity by deciding beforehand what will need doing in order to successfully complete the task, and deciding on assessment criteria for judging the success of their work and for setting directing/managing targets for the future.

Each group now scripts their improvisation with the objective that the script must give enough detail for another group to be able to perform it exactly as the writing group intended. Each group is given the following template for their script that they must keep to:

- ten lines of speech (single sentences or exchanges according to ability)
- five stage directions
- two significant props
- one 'dramatic' pause.

Teacher works with each group helping them to develop their ideas within the constraints and modelling, where appropriate, how to use speech to convey stage directions, and how to use stage directions to convey aspects of character.

> The constraints of a given number of lines and stage directions are intended to introduce a game element and also to encourage pupils to be selective and economical with the actions and words needed to convey situation, character and mood. The limits set also ensure that this is a manageable task in terms of time and energy for writing in drama.

When they have completed their tasks, groups either word-process or copy scripts onto large sheets of paper. The scripts are then rotated so that each group gets another's script to work on.

Episode 5   From page to stage

Groups allocate roles of actors and directors and decide on how to rehearse their piece – the group might subdivide into two groups of two actors and a director, for instance, and then compare interpretations. The groups can only use the script as it has been given to them; they cannot add or take away anything.

> This rule serves several purposes. Having to stick to another group's original text will prompt the group to discuss the writers' intentions and the problems of faithfully reproducing the actions and words in performance. Often groups will want to add further stage directions and movement – this should be resisted because sometimes groups may discover that less movement/action creates a more powerful effect. The writing group are also offered a clear demonstration of the strengths and limitations of their original script.

After rehearsing, each group presents their scene. The teacher encourages discussion between the acting and writing groups about the script, so that the class consider both the needs and intentions of writers, actors and directors when working on scripts. Teacher explains the differences between a 'faithful' representation of a script and an 'interpretive' approach and asks the acting group how they might have done the scene differently if they had been allowed to add their own dialogue and/or stage directions. The writing group are asked what changes they might now want to make to their script, having seen it performed.

The whole class reflect on the devising process so far and how themes, tensions, characters and ideas are developing.

Extensions

The written scenes might become the 'anchors' or key scenes for use in a continuing devising process, which uses a variety of dramatic techniques to further explore character, themes and plot. The class select from this work to create a performance, which includes scripted scenes and other performance devices such as tableaux, thought tracking, sound tracking, alter-ego, flashbacks, etc.

Year 9 – The shaping of identity

Rationale

This sequence of lessons builds on the skills and understandings of devising developed in Years 7 and 8. Here, pupils begin a more complex process of constructing a fully developed character based on their social and aesthetic explorations of the people and other influences that shape our identities. This work also encourages pupils to question familiar forms of character representation and their own sense of 'self' and 'other'. Pupils are also encouraged to adapt and develop filmic devices and technology in their work. For pupils going on to GCSE, this is a good opportunity to evaluate their skills in devising and performing. For all pupils it is an opportunity to close Year 9 with a sequence which encourages critical thinking and public debate about identity and the shaping of identity.

Resources

Three hours of class time and one homework
Flipchart/board and markers
Copies of the stimulus
Basic stage properties and costume as needed
CD player
Digital camera, data projector and Powerpoint, if available

Specialist and framework objectives

Specialist Learning Strand objectives: Acting/Inter-Acting	A4: play a wide range of characters in different styles based on research, observation and personal interpretation IA1: work as part of an ensemble – acting and re-acting to others
Directing/Managing	D1: make creative and symbolic use of the elements of drama from pupils' own experience of drama and from watching drama M3: ask for and act on information, opinions, feelings and ideas from others
Reviewing/Evaluating	R5: evaluate and analyse the structure, meaning and impact of plays studied, watched or taken part in E2: develop critical thinking about texts, issues and situations through work in role
Framework objectives: Drama	SL11: recognise, evaluate and extend the skills and techniques developed through drama SL12: use a range of drama techniques to explore issues, ideas and meanings

S&L	SL10: contribute to organisation of group activity in ways that help to structure plans, solve problems and evaluate alternatives
Reading	TR7: compare the presentation of ideas, values or emotions in related or contrasting texts
Writing	TW5: explore ways of opening, structuring and ending narratives and experiment with narrative perspective

Selected specialist teaching approaches

- Use a variety of techniques and conventions to explore character, settings and plot though drama rather than through discussion.

- Encourage and reward pupils' responses which are experimental and non-realist in terms of the use of body and voice.

- Ensure that pupils respond to each other's work at various stages of development using appropriate tone and vocabulary.

- Identify and use examples of good work as models for other groups to follow.

- Model activities which challenge the pupils and demand co-operation and negotiation in paired and small-group work.

- Create opportunities for critical reflection so that pupils think about and articulate their insights from the drama experience.

- Challenge pupils to take responsibility for a dramatic idea by suggesting that they lead others in the exploration.

Performance indicators

During the sequence of lessons, pupils always/sometimes/rarely:

- initiate, explore and experiment with new ideas and ways of making;
- perform in a range of styles and genres conveying different emotions and effects;
- can explain how costume, setting and technical effects may change audience response, mood and atmosphere;
- work constructively with others to shape performances that offer new insights into issues and ideas;
- are aware of the way texts are mediated and offer particular perspectives (voice); and
- use voice and movement to create and portray characters that maintain an audience's interest.

Stimulus

And one man in his time plays many parts,
His acts being seven ages. At first the infant,
Mewing and puking in the nurse's arms.
And then the whining schoolboy, with his satchel,
And shining morning face, creeping like snail
Unwillingly to school. And then the lover,
Sighing like furnace, with a woeful ballad
Made to his mistress' eyebrow. Then a soldier,
Full of strange oaths, and bearded like the pard,
Jealous in honour, sudden and quick in quarrel,
Seeking the double reputation
Even in the cannon's mouth. And then the justice,
In fair round belly with good capon lin'd
With eyes severe, and beard of formal cut,
Full of wise saws and modern instances;
And so he plays his part. The sixth age shifts
Into the lean and slipper'd pantaloon,
With spectacles on nose and pouch on side,
His youthful hose well sav'd a world too wide
For his shrunk shank; and his big manly voice,
Turning again towards childish treble, pipes
And whistles in his sound. Last scene of all,
That ends this strange eventful history,
Is second childishness, and mere oblivion,
Sans teeth, sans eyes, sans taste, sans everything
– *As You Like It*

1.

Solomon Grundy

Solomon Grundy
Born on Monday,
Christened on Tuesday
Married on Wednesday
Took ill on Thursday,
Worse on Friday
Died on Saturday
Buried on Sunday
That was the end of Solomon Grundy.

2.

Josephine Jacobie

Josephine Jacobie
Born on a Monday
Seduced on Tuesday
Feller left Wednesday
They put her out Thursday
She get a job Friday
The money done Saturday
She cry all Sunday
The baby born Monday
What do you think they call the baby?
Josephine Jacobie

3.

Teaching Episode 1 The rhythm of life

Teacher explains objectives for the sequence of lessons, which are to explore issues related to the shaping of identity at different stages of our lives, and to use this exploration to create a fully developed central character and her relationship with other significant characters who have played a part in shaping her identity. The outcome of the work will be a devised performance using a variety of narrative techniques and filmic devices.

The teacher begins with copies of Jacques' speech from *As You Like It*. Teacher reads and checks any words not understood. In groups, class are asked to look at the speech and try to work out what the seven stages are and how man is pictured by Shakespeare at that stage of life – what picture does he paint of old age, for instance?

> Depending on circumstances and group, the teacher might energise this discussion by having the pupils make a standing circle and asking for one volunteer to enter the circle and imitate/caricature man for each of the different stages of life, as teacher gives an expressive/performed second reading of the text. Volunteers should self-select as the text is read and return to the circle when they have had their go. Alternatively, the whole class could be moving and responding to Shakespeare's images.

Groups are given two questions for discussion and feedback to the class:

- Can you still recognise these seven stages of man in our own time, or have things changed?
- Do we all go through the same stages of life, or are we all too different from each other?

Teacher leads class discussion based on responses from groups and also draws attention to the cycle in Shakespeare's text, which goes from childhood to 'second childishness'.

Teacher introduces *Solomon Grundy* and asks class to consider how this poem is the same/different from the Shakespeare text. Why is this poem so well known in the English culture of nursery rhymes? Teacher also draws attention to the rhythm of the rhyme and asks whether this is part of its appeal.

Finally, teacher introduces *Josephine Jacobie,* a modern rhyme based on *Solomon Grundy*. In groups, class consider the following questions and give feedback to the class.

> These questions are there to prompt discussion. What is of real interest is how do we, class and teacher, begin to construct 'Josephine Jacobie' in our imaginations. What does the poem influence us to assume in terms of her class, family and cultural upbringing, her intelligence – how she is made? What do our imaginings tell us about us? Why do we imagine her in the ways we do? How different is Josephine from us? These are important issues for pupils to discuss and consider in public. The teacher needs to sensitively lead the discussion and feedback from the questions asked into reflections on our sense of 'self' and 'other'. This kind of reality check can usefully be returned to at appropriate moments as the work progresses.

- Do all girls/women go through these stages? If not, what kind of girls do?

- Why do 'they' call the baby Josephine Jacobie in the last line?

- What might stop Josephine Jacobie's baby from repeating the same cycle of experiences as her mother?

- Is the poem a warning to other girls like Josephine? If so, what is the message?

Teacher manages class making a collective role-on-the-wall for 'Josephine Jacobie', using prompts such as:

What kind of girl is she?

What do you imagine her family/school background is?

What's in her heart?

How do other people see her?

What questions do you want to ask her?

Class divides into groups and teacher explains the first drama exercise which is to find a way of performing the poem using vocal rhythms accompanied by simple physical gestures for each day in Josephine's 'week'. Teacher models some choices for working with the rhythm of the poem – clapping, rap, rounds – and asks for examples of gestures to go with particular days. A further objective is set, which is to try and find a way of communicating the cycle of Josephine's life, i.e. her baby will be the same as her and have the same cycle of experiences. During the group work, the teacher looks out for examples of good ideas emerging from the work and stops the class to point these out as appropriate.

> This is an opportunity for some high-energy work for voices and bodies! Pupils should be encouraged to keep the work really pacy and physical.

The class share their work and teacher selects individuals to comment on the strengths and effects of each group's work as well as pointers for further development or emphasis.

Episode 2 Josephine's hopes and fears

Teacher organises class into eight groups of three (one group for each day of the week), and each group makes a core image for their day. They can use two actors in the image; the third pupil serves as the director. The director's role is to lead a discussion with the actors about which moment in the day to isolate and work on for the image. How can one image be selected and made so that it 'speaks' for the whole day? The discussion also includes how to make best use of the second actor to create tension or to make a point about Josephine's experiences on that day. The director then works with the actors to create the image, and position it for maximum effect for an audience.

> This assumes 24 pupils which is of course a rather small Year 9 class. Either repeat certain days so that you have different versions to compare, or add extra actors/directors to each of the eight groups.

When the groups are ready, the teacher claps hands to signal each group to show its image. All the images stay in place until the end. All the pupils who are not playing Josephine then step out. The teacher then asks each of the Josephines in turn: *'What is your hope?'* (or *'What do you hope for?'*) and *'What is your fear?'* A volunteer enters Josephine's answers onto the role-on-the-wall.

The other characters are now placed on chairs in the centre of a circle and hot-seated by other pupils in order to find out about their perspective of Josephine and the events of the day.

Following feedback and discussion of issues, ideas and themes raised by responses to questioning the Josephine roles about their hopes and fears and hot-seating the other characters, class have second opportunity to add to Josephine's role-on-the-wall using the same prompts as before.

Episode 3   Songs and symbols of the week

In same groups, pupils make or find a significant object that symbolises that day and decide what song is playing on the radio. Teacher encourages the class to play with ironies, so that there may be an emotional difference between the object and the song – placing a teddy bear with a broken arm against Stevie Wonder's *Happy Birthday to Ya* for the Monday for instance.

> Objects include all kinds of text, of course – letters, cards, memos, photos, posters, novels, poems. Written or crafted texts/objects have a double purpose: they have to be constructed/written and then they also serve as objects or properties in drama space or world – they change the landscape as well as containing their own message.

When they are ready, all the objects are positioned carefully for effect in the centre of a large circle. The teacher describes how the sharing will look like the opening of a film with the camera moving across various objects as soundtracks fade in and out. As everyone focuses on the object of the first day, that group begins to sing the song they have chosen with everyone in the large group joining in. Continue around through all the days. When all the songs have been sung, pupils move closer to examine the objects and/or ask questions of the makers of the objects.

> This exercise is deliberately focused on one of the three key principles of progression discussed in Section 1 – becoming more selective and complex in their use of sign and gesture to make and represent meanings. Here the pupils must carefully select objects, consider how they are placed, what music will be placed with/against the object and how to give this montage character – how to make the object and music speak for the character, tell us more about who she is and what is happening to her.

Alternatively, each group is given the opportunity to take a single image or multiple images of the object in its setting using digital camera or a short video. The task here is to think in terms of film and how to use camera shot and perspective to maximise the dramatic effect of the chosen object. Each group then finds an MP3 of their chosen song and use Powerpoint to present their image with soundtrack.

> This task adds further dimensions to the challenge of being selective and complex. Here pupils must also select how the audience sees the montage and how they will be positioned in relation to the montage.

Episode 4 Josephine in the eye of the storm

Teacher reorganises class into five new groups. Each group is given the task of creating a naturalistic scene for one of the five days of the week selected by the teacher or negotiated with class. Again, the task demands that the pupils isolate one scene from all the possibles they can imagine for their day that will effectively 'speak' for, or sum up, the events and experiences of the whole day.

The teacher explains that there are further constraints and objectives for the group to consider. The scene is to start at a moment right after 'a storm has passed'. However, even though it appears calm, there must be some subtle, significant action that suggests the further storm, which is still to come. In other words, this is a scene which takes place in the 'eye of the storm'.

The actions and words that the group use to build up the tension of another storm brewing must be connected with Josephine's surrendering of herself. In other words, it must show, to some degree, the responsibility that Josephine has for what is happening to her and how she is contributing to her own process of victimization. As the scenes are shared, the teacher asks the pupils to pinpoint the moments where they feel she is surrendering herself and could have stood up for herself more, or done something to change her situation.

> The poem makes Josephine passive. Others do things to her. This reality check is to do with reminding ourselves that we have a role to play in shaping our identities as well – we may learn to be one way but we can always re-learn and change. If the focus is on the personal and social importance of this theme, then pupils might use forum theatre to interrogate key moments in each scene and suggest words and actions that Josephine might change to stop the process of victimisation. The rest of the class can comment on Josephine's potential for these changes.

Episode 5   What do they call her?

Teacher works with class to create an image of Josephine just after she has given birth to her child. If an appropriate image has already been produced in earlier work, this could be re-made and used. If not, the teacher asks for a volunteer to be modelled by the rest of the class – they should also position the baby in the image and so suggest what Josephine's reaction is to the child. Does she hold it? Does she turn away from it? Pupils are asked to explain the suggestions they make as they position and reposition the models of Josephine and her baby. When the class has finished, the teacher offers the pupil being modelled as Josephine the chance to make up her own mind based on the suggestions made by the group and, at a given signal, the pupil decides and forms her own image of mother and baby. Class reflect on her choice and their response to it.

The teacher asks the class to imagine who else might be in the hospital ward. What does Josephine notice as she lies there? What does she learn about herself and the world from what she sees and hears around her?

Teacher invites class, one by one, to take up a position in role as someone who is in the ward at this moment. As they take position they must give themselves a caption such as: *'I am the young nurse giving out pills to the patients'* or *'I am a proud father visiting my baby's mother'*. When all are in place, teacher asks some of the characters: *'When you look at Josephine Jacobie, what do you see? When she looks at you, how will she see you?'*

> Its not necessary for everyone to contribute unless they want to. A selection of potential characters and tensions will be enough as the basis for forming groups to further explore and extend the ideas offered here.

The class brainstorm possibilities of other characters, events and images. Teacher asks for groups of volunteers to take responsibility for realising some of these ideas. The teacher explains that this will be a whole-class presentation – again in the style of a sequence in a film, which takes us into the ward and selects images and words for the viewer.

When the groups are ready they consider, as a class, how to choreograph their work to maximum effect – who goes first? Should the 'camera' move down the ward or move from place to place? When these agreements have been made, the teacher takes up position as Josephine and the class perform their work around her.

As the performance finishes, the teacher narrates: *'Josephine looks directly into the camera and speaks to the audience – what does she say to them? What has she learnt? What does she want for her baby? Who is she?'*

Teacher asks which of the other characters we have met during the work are not present at the birth. Where are they now as Josephine speaks? Class decide and place characters and suggest their context of place and situation.

> This can be done quickly by keeping the class together and asking anyone who has an idea to take volunteers and whatever else they need and make the image they have in mind there and then. This can be repeated till all the other characters are placed.

Class return to the role-on-the-wall and add to it. In groups, pupils write Josephine's monologue which is a direct address to the audience about her life/situation and what she has learnt/not learnt from her experiences. When the monologue is performed, the 'other' characters will be positioned in the space so that Josephine has the opportunity to move around and use the images of the other characters in her performance of the monologue.

When the monologues have been prepared and rehearsed, the space is rearranged with the 'bed' in the ward and the images of where the other characters are in place, then each of the Josephines takes up a starting position, performs the monologue and returns to his/her starting position as a signal for the next actor to begin, until all are performed.

Extensions

Joseph Jacobie: In four groups of six, pupils write the ditty for Joseph Jacobie and perform it with a gesture accompanying each line. Reflect on and discuss the different ways in which we construct Joseph and Josephine and what that tells us.

The work developed here may form the core of a devised performance with the class of the shaping of identity, or different gender expectations of how young people grow and develop, or bi-gender adolescent relationships.

An A–Z of drama conventions and techniques

This is a collection of frequently used conventions and techniques for structuring drama, simply arranged in alphabetical order. References to these techniques are frequently made in drama teaching texts, policy and curriculum documents. The conventions are not structures in themselves; they are more like the building blocks or palette that is used, alongside others, to create structures. Cookery is a useful analogy here. The list of conventions is like the list of ingredients for a recipe. It is only when the 'ingredients' are combined and subtly blended that they become a satisfying meal (montage)! I have only given here a brief definition of the most popular conventions. For further explanation of the conventions and the conventions approach to structuring, see Neelands, J. (ed. Goode, T.) 1990 *Structuring Drama Work*: Cambridge University Press.

Alter-ego	This involves a pupil other than the one playing the character as an extension of that character. The alter-ego's main function is to express the *feelings* or 'inner speech' of the character. This convention is designed to deepen the collective understanding of how a character might be feeling about a given situation, even though the character itself may not be able to express those feelings (text/sub-text). The expression of feeling may be verbal or physical. Very effective when used in conjunction with hot-seating.
Choral speak	A written text is divided up and spoken by group. Text may be dramatic or otherwise. The construction of the choral speak should comment on, or develop, the original text rather than literally follow the line divisions or allocation of lines to single characters. Particularly effective when the choral speak is part of a montage with another convention, e.g. tableau, or mime.
Circular drama	A variation on *small-group drama*, in which groups are given different scenes involving a central character. The groups prepare the scene and then the *teacher in role* joins each scene as the central character and improvises briefly with each group before moving on. This provides the opportunity to see the different ways in which the central character reacts in a variety of public and private contexts.
Collective character	A character is improvised by a group of pupils; any one of them can speak as the character. In this way the whole class can be involved in a dialogue, for instance, by half the class taking on one of the characters involved. There

doesn't need to be conformity in the responses they make; different attitudes can be given expression so that there is also dialogue between members of the collective character.

Come on down! Any popular game show format is used if it can either illuminate or make ironic the events and characters. Chat-show formats provide an alternative form of *hot-seating*; pupils should identify and preserve the generic features of the game show in their work.

Conflicting advice Characters are offered conflicting advice as to what to do about any given situation. This can be done in character by other characters in the drama, and by voices in the character's head played by other members of the group. It is possible to develop this convention by allowing the character to engage in conversation with the voices and thus challenge the advice being offered. Also, the voices themselves may engage in debate with the character listening in.

Conscience alley At a critical moment in a character's life, when a dilemma, problem, or choice must be made, the character walks between two rows of pupils who may offer advice as the character passes. The advice may be from the pupils as themselves or from other characters; the advice may include lines or words spoken earlier in the drama.

Defining space The drama space is carefully marked out into different locations or times. A key space in the drama, such as a particular room, is reconstructed using available props and furniture.

Documentary The events of the drama are translated into a documentary format, or characters are established through documentary evidence, cf. *Citizen Kane.*

Flashback The relationship between the dramatic present and the past is reinforced by showing 'flashback' scenes while the present scene unfolds, or at a crucial moment a character is confronted by images of the past.

Forum theatre A small group act out a drama for the rest of the group as 'observers'. Both the 'performers' and the 'observers' have the right to stop the drama at any point and make suggestions as to how it might proceed; ask for it to be replayed with changes designed to bring out another point of view or focus; deepen the drama by using any of the other conventions. An important feature is that all the participants, 'performers' and 'observers' take responsibility for the crafting of the drama – the responsibility does not lie solely with the 'performers'; in fact, they are more like puppets responding to their puppeteers.

Gestus Pupils present a dramatic sequence which includes a specially loaded action or gesture – something that the audience sees which clearly relates to the broader theme or historical context of the whole performance text, as well as belonging to the immediate context the pupils are creating. A ring that cannot be made to fit; a doll that is carelessly dropped by a negligent parent; a murderer trying to wash her hands.

Gossip circle	The private and public behaviour of characters is commented on in the form of rumours and gossip circulating in the community; as the rumours 'spread' around the circle they become exaggerated and distorted. A useful way of identifying tensions, conflicts and contradictions for further exploration.
Group sculpture	The group, or an individual from the group, models volunteers into a shape, usually of a non-representational nature, which expresses a particular aspect of the theme or issue being addressed. The collective creation of this 'sculpture' will force the group members to bring out their own, individual interpretation of events portrayed in the drama. This is not to be confused with *tableaux* which tend to be literal representations.
Headlines	Statements in the style of newspaper headlines are used to focus the attention on to a particular aspect of the drama. Used with *tableaux* several headlines can be given for the same photograph in order to highlight different points of view and bias.
Hot-seating	Characters are questioned about their values, motives, relationships and actions by other members of the group. This is a very effective rehearsal technique that helps an actor to flesh out and discover new facets of their character through the responses they make to the questions. The questioners may also be in role as witnesses, historians, detectives, etc. There can be added tension if the character is questioned at a moment of stress, or at a turning point in their lives.
Iceberg	A reflective device in which a diagram of an iceberg is drawn. Pupils have to consider what is text and what is sub-text in a scene and then to note text above the waterline of the iceberg and sub-text beneath the waterline.
Improvisation	A spontaneous acting out of a given situation in which pupils have to respond to the given circumstances – who, where, when, what. An unscripted performance or a situation is prepared by one group of pupils and then is improvised with the teacher-in-role or with volunteers from another group.
Interviews, interrogations	Characters are interviewed by 'reporters' or interrogated by an authority figure in order to question their motives, values and beliefs or to elicit more facts about a given situation.
Letters	Delivered by the teacher/leader to either the whole group or to small sub-groups in order to introduce a new idea, focus or tension to the existing drama. The participants can write them both in and out of character as a means of crystallising thought or reflecting on past action.
Mantle of the expert	The major feature of this convention is that the pupils are in role as characters with specialist knowledge relevant to the situation they find themselves in. In its purest form, mantle of the expert requires an approach to teaching and learning that is holistic and therefore cross-curricular; however, I have found that endowing pupils with expertise is in itself extremely powerful, motivating and empowering.

Marking the moment	Allows the participants to reflect on a time within the drama in which strong reactions, emotions or feelings were felt by the individuals within the group. They are reflecting out of character and so the reactions identified are those of the participants themselves, not the characters they were playing. They use any of the other conventions suitable for sharing their moment with the rest of the group.
Meetings	The group get together in order to address some problem or to discuss information within the format of a formal meeting, which may be further controlled by the local cultural circumstances of the fiction: power and status of characters, for instance. This is also very useful for the teacher to input information, create atmosphere or inject tension within the fiction, rather than stopping the drama in order to do so.
Moment of truth	A technique in which the group must devise a final scene for the drama. They must engage in reflective discussion of the major events and tensions in order to create a sharp focus for the final scene.
Narration	One of the participants tells the story while the others 'act it out', or a series of scenes are linked by narrative which can either simply tell the story or, more importantly, comment on the action from a particular point of view.
Overheard conversations	The group 'listen in' to 'private' conversations between characters in the drama. An interesting and challenging development of this is for the group to agree whether or not the information gained from listening in can be used in the subsequent drama, or is it something they must pretend not to know. By enabling the participants to listen in to a private conversation, the teacher/leader can introduce a new idea, or a threat or problem, by creating rumour that will be interpreted in a variety of ways.
Private property	A character is introduced, or constructed, through carefully chosen personal belongings – objects, letters, reports, costume, toys, medals, etc. The intimacy of the information gleaned from these objects may be contrasted with a character who reveals very little about themselves or who presents a contradictory self-image from that suggested by the objects – the private property forms a sub-text to the character's words and actions.
Re-enactments	In order to examine a situation in more detail, a scene or an event that has 'already happened' may be re-enacted. If this is linked into the idea of clarification of fact or confirmation of the source of a rumour, it can provide a very powerful focus for checking and confirming the whole group's growing understanding of a given situation.
Reportage	Participants report on a situation in the style of a journalist, either from within the drama in character or outside of it out of character. The journalist can work in any media form.
Ritual and ceremony	Pupils create appropriate rituals and ceremonies that might be celebrated or endured by characters to mark anniversaries, cycles, initiations, belief systems, etc.

Role on the wall	A record of a character is kept in the form of a large outline of a figure in which pupils might write key lines, phrases, ideas or feelings about the character. The outline is kept and re-edited as pupils discover more about the character.
Small-group drama	Sub-groups of the whole class work on separate but related interpretations or developments of the major theme.
Soundtracking	Sounds are used to create the atmosphere of the 'place' in which the drama takes place. These can be prerecorded or live and are usually, though not always, created by the participants.
Space between	Pupils arrange characters so that the space between them represents the distance in their relationship to each other (how near and far apart, who is close to whom). The pupils can also consider the change in the space over time – will characters draw closer together or further apart? They can also try to name the distance – betrayal, fear, power, etc.
Split-screen	Pupils plan two or more scenes which occur in different times and places; they then work on cutting backwards and forwards between the two scenes as in film/TV. The edit of the two scenes should be carefully prepared to maximise the links, analogies or irony between the two.
Tableau	Participants create a physical image using their own bodies to represent a moment from the drama. Combined with *soundtracking, thought tracking,* this convention can be used in a variety of different circumstances. Try linking two or more together as a way of developing a narrative sequence or predicting possible outcomes.
Teacher in role	Expressed in its simplest form, the teacher/leader takes part in the drama along with the other participants. Teachers often feel extremely reticent, for a variety of reasons, about joining in alongside the pupils but there is no doubt at all that they respond very positively indeed to their teacher becoming part of the shared act of creating a drama.
Telephone conversations	The listeners hear either one side of the conversation only or both sides, depending on the intention of their using the convention. The teacher/leader can also use this to add information, develop the narrative or inject tension from within the fiction.
This way – that way	The same scene or events can be played with different narrators; the playing of the scene will be subtly altered according to the narrator's interests and perspective.
Thought tracking	The inner thoughts of a character are revealed either by the person adopting that role or by the others in the group. This is a particularly useful way of slowing down and deepening a drama, especially it used in conjunction with *tableaux*.
Unfinished materials	The group is presented with a piece of writing, drawing, diagram, audio or videotape which is incomplete. Their task is to complete it or solve the problem of why it has not been finished.

Venting   A variation on *thought tracking* in which pupils can come up and vent the feelings, emotions, confusions, ambiguities in the character's mind at that moment. Several pupils can vent simultaneously to create a 'dialogue' or to demonstrate different views of the character's state of mind.

Whole-group drama   All of the participants including, usually, the teacher/leader, are engaged in the same drama at the same time (see also *meetings*).

Bibliography

The rationale/philosophy of drama education

Boal, A. (1994) *The Rainbow of Desire*. Routledge.

Bolton, G. (1984) *Drama as Education: An argument for placing drama at the centre of the curriculum*. Longman.

Bolton, G. (1992) *New Perspectives on Classroom Drama*. Simon & Schuster.

Gallagher, K. (2000) *Drama Education in the Lives of Girls*. University of Toronto Press.

Hornbrook, D. (1991) *Education in Drama*. Falmer Press.

Hornbrook, D. (2000) *Education and Dramatic Art* (2nd Edition). Routledge.

Johnson, L. and O'Neill, D. (1984) *Dorothy Heathcote: Collected Writings on Education and Drama*. Hutchinson.

McGregor, L. *et al.* (1977) *Learning through Drama*. Heinemann.

Nicholson, H (ed.) (2000) *Teaching Drama 11–18*. Continuum.

O'Neill, C. (1995) *Drama Worlds*. Heinemann US.

O'Toole, J. (1992) *The Process of Drama*. Routledge.

Taylor, P. (2000) *The Drama Classroom: Action, reflection, transformation*. Routledge.

Wagner, B. J. (1972) *Drama as a Learning Medium*. Hutchinson.

Strategies/approachs for teaching drama at KS3

Bowell, P. and Heap, B.S. (2001) *Planning Process Drama*, David Fulton. An accessible guide for planning and teaching process drama (otherwise known as 'living through' drama), an improvisational drama form focused on particpants' learning.

Clarke, J. *et al.* (1997) *Lessons for the Living: Drama in the transition years*. Mayfair (Canada). An accessible and useful series of lesson structures and advice on planning and teaching specially designed for KS3.

Crinson, J. and Leake, L. (ed.) (1993) *Move Back the Desks*. NATE. An excellent publication giving case studies of drama work in English and guidance in managing drama.

Fleming, M. (1995) *Starting Drama Teaching*. David Fulton. A crucial introduction for drama teachers which combines some rationale with numerous concrete strategies.

Fleming, M. (2001) *Teaching Drama in Primary and Secondary Schools*. David Fulton. Chapters 1–4 will be of particular interest. Fleming offers a combination of theory and practice, situated within a view of drama over the last two decades.

James, R. and Williams, P. (1980) *A Guide to Improvisation*. Kemble Press. Gradual, simple and protected steps into the drama teaching situation, offering exercises in verbal and non-verbal drama form.

Kempe, A. and Ashwell, M. (2000) *Progression in Secondary Drama*. Heinemann. A very useful and detailed framework for an 11–18 drama curriculum with a clear stress on planning for progression. Full of suggestions and schemes of work.

Lyon, L., Nicholson, H., Rooke, C. and Wrigley, D. (2000) *The National Drama Secondary Drama Teacher's Handbook*. National Drama Publications. A practical guide for HoDs and teachers with responsibility for managing drama. Advice on planning, assesment and other departmental policy-making.

Morgan, N. and Saxton, J. (1987) *Teaching Drama*. Hutchinson. Through consideration of the nature and types of drama teaching, this book offers approaches and strategies for drama work which can be applied to material selected by the teacher.

Neelands, J. (1984) *Making Sense of Drama*. Heinemann. Although dated in parts, Chapters 3–8 concisely deal with important basic considerations for the approach of the drama teacher, synthesising the work of many educational practitioners.

Neelands, J. (1992) *Learning through Imagined Experience*. Hodder & Stoughton. A range of strategies which highlight both the value and the possible approaches for introducing learning through drama into the classroom in the context of English in the National Curriculum.

Neelands, J. and Goode, T. (2000) *Structuring Dramawork* (2nd Edition). Cambridge University Press. This book defines a range of theatre/drama conventions and principles for structuring and developing drama work and drama-based learning.

O'Neill, C. and Lambert, A. (1982) *Drama Structures*. Hutchinson. A trusted reference text for shaping and developing material for drama work.

Smith, K. (1986) *Stages in Drama*. Foulsham. A real mixture of drama/theatre lesson plans. Intended as a stopgap for non-specialist drama teachers and for cover lessons.

Taylor, K. (1990) *Drama Strategies*. London Drama. Sample lesson plans and basic strategies for drama, devised by groups of London teachers.

Taylor, P. (1998) *Redcoats and Patriots: Reflective practice in drama and social studies*. Heinemann US. Considers the role of drama in social studies through the eyes of a teacher who is introducing these appoaches in his classroom.

Winston, J. and Tandy, M. (2000) *Beginning Drama 4–11*. David Fulton.

Beyond KS3

Cooper, S. and Mackey, S. (2000) *Drama and Theatre Studies* (2nd Edition) Nelson Thornes. A manual on drama and theatre studies, designed for AS and A2 specifications in the subject. This new edition contains three main sections: 'Exploring Texts', 'Reviewing Productions' and 'Key Practitioners'. There are test questions, exam-style activities, and bibliographies.

Cross, D. and Reynolds, C. (2001) *GCSE Drama for OCR*. Heinemann. A syllabus-specific guide to coursework and other projects.

Fleming, M. (1997) *The Art of Drama Teaching*. David Fulton. Explores a variety of theatre conventions through extracts from dramatic literature and exercises.

Kempe, A. (1999) *The GCSE Drama Coursebook* (2nd Edition), Blackwell. Primarily a series of lesson plans from which approaches can be extracted. Uses literary (playtexts) as sample resources for drama work.

Kempe, A. and Warner, L. (1997) *Starting with Scripts*. Stanley Thornes. Offering an approach to secondary-school drama that examines the script as a blueprint for performance, this book gives strategies for tackling the subject in accordance with National Curriculum requirements. The content is structured so that all elements of the theatrical process are covered, giving pupils a picture of the context in which theatre is produced.

Lamsden, G. (2000) *Devising*. Hodder & Stoughton. The aim of this concise handbook is to demystify the devising process. The emphasis of the text is upon the development of good devising skills to enable pupils to succeed in the devising part of their course. Step-by-step activities help pupils to explore the process and build their confidence, and information on major practitioners is included. Case studies from professional devising companies put study into context.

Mackey, S. (ed.) (2000) *Practical Theatre*. Nelson Thornes. Serving as a companion volume to Cooper and Mackey (2000), this book provides detailed coverage of the practical aspects of the A-Level Theatre Studies/Performing Arts syllabuses and GNVQ Performing Arts. Drawing on the expertise of a wide range of practitioners, with sections on practical theatre, support and technology, and enabling theatre.

Morton, J. (2001) *AQA GCSE Drama*. A syllabus-specific guide to coursework and other projects.

Neelands, J. and Dobson, W. (2000) *Drama and Theatre Studies at A/S and A Level*. Hodder & Stoughton. This text aims to provide an essential manual for AS/A-Level pupils of drama and theatre studies. The text provides advice, information and exercises to help pupils study and make theatre, and the user-friendly text with illustrations, extensive glossary and highlighted key points aids the learning process.

Neelands, J. and Dobson, W. (2000) *Theatre Directions*. Hodder & Stoughton. This text looks at the diverse influences on theatre through first-hand accounts from major theatre practitioners. It contains writings from more than 20 key dramatists, including Aristotle, Artaud, Brecht, Grotowski, Kazan, Stanislavski, Strindberg and Zola.

O'Toole, J. and Haseman, B. (1987) *Dramawise*. Heinemann. Intended as a kind of coursework book for GCSE groups, the sections in this book offer a developing picture of elements of drama using a range of sources in project form.

Taylor, K. and Leeder, J. (2001) *EDEXCEL GCSE Drama*. Hodder. This syllabus-specific title examines numerous drama forms and provides pupils with a knowledge and understanding of drama and theatre within a social, cultural and historical context. In addition, it offers full support for ICT, Key Skills and Citizenship requirements within drama.

Teaching Shakespeare

Ackroyd, J. *et al.* (1998) *Key Shakespeare Book 1.* Hodder.
Gilmour, M. (ed.) (1997) *Shakespeare for All in the Primary School.* Cassell.
Gilmour, M. (1997) *Shakespeare in Secondary Schools.* Cassell.
Leach, S. (1992) *Shakespeare in the Classroom.* Open University Press.
O'Brien, V. (1982) *Teaching Shakespeare.* Edward Arnold.
Pinder, B. (1992) *Shakespeare: An active approach.* Unwin Hyman.

Drama games

Brandes, D. and Phillips, H. (1978) *Gamester's Handbook* (140 Games for teachers and Group Leaders). Hutchinson.
Brandes, D. (1982) *Gamester's Handbook Two.* Hutchinson.
Scher, A. and Verrall, C. (1975) *100+ Ideas for Drama.* Heinemann.
Scher, A. and Verrall, C. (1975) *Another 100+ Ideas for Drama.* Heinemann.

Theatre/actor training

Barker, C. (1977) *Theatre Games.* Methuen.
Boal, A. (1992) *Games for Actors and Non-actors.* Routledge.
Callow, S. (1984) *Being an Actor.* Penguin.
Harrop, J. (1992) *Acting.* Routledge.
Hodgson, J. and Richards, E. (1966) *Improvisation.* Eyre Methuen.
Johnstone, K. (1979) *Impro.* Methuen.
Miles-Brown, J. (1985) *Acting: A drama studio source book.* Peter Owen.

Modern theatre texts and performance theory

Artaud, A. (1970) *The Theatre and its Double.* Calder & Boyars.
Aston, E. and Savona, G. (1992) *Theatre as Sign System.* Routledge.
Barba, E. and Savarese, N. (1991) *A Dictionary of Theatre Anthropology: The secret art of the performer.* Routledge.
Beckerman, B. (1990) *Theatrical Presentation.* Routledge.
Boal, A. (1979) *Theatre of the Oppressed.* Pluto Press.
Braun, E. (1982) *The Director and the Stage: From Naturalism to Grotowski.* Methuen.
Brook, P. (1968) *The Empty Space.* Penguin.
Brook, P. (1987) *The Shifting Point.* Methuen.
Carlson, M. (1996) *Performance: A critical introduction.* Routledge.
Counsell, C. (1996) *Signs of Performance: A history of twentieth-century theatre.* Routledge.

Drain, R. (1995) *Twentieth Century Theatre: A reader*. Routledge.

Esslin, M. (1987) *The Field of Drama*. Methuen.

Fuegi, J. (1987) *Bertolt Brecht: Chaos according to plan*. Cambridge University Press.

Grotowski, J. (1969) *Towards a Poor Theatre*. Methuen.

Magarshack, D. *Stanislavski: A Life*. Methuen.

Schechner, R. (1988) *Performance Theory*. University Paperbacks.

Schechner, R. (2001) *Performance Studies: An introduction*. Routledge.

Styan, J. L. (1978) *Modern Drama in Theory and Practice: Part 1 – Naturalism and Realism*. Cambridge University Press.

Styan, J. L. (1978) *Modern Drama in Theory and Practice: Part 2 – Symbolism, surrealism and the absurd*. Cambridge University Press.

Styan, J.L. (1978) *Modern Drama in Theory and Practice: Part 3 – Expressionism and epic theatre*. Cambridge University Press.

Willet, J. (ed.) (1964) *Brecht on Theatre*. Methuen.

Williams, R. (1968) *Drama from Ibsen to Brecht*. Methuen.

Index